Doc Jackson's Letters Home:

A Combat Medic's 1968 Letters from Vietnam

Private E-1 Jerome Jackson's letters, hurriedly handwritten on muddy paper to his mother from jungles and sandbag bunkers, tell the true, first person, contemporary account of a combat medic, rich with the details of how soldiers survived day to day in a life-threatening landscape. They reveal Doc's rage against the mismanagement of a military fiasco during what Jackson considered a senseless war. The letters were discovered in his mother's estate. Interspersed are related recollections as told from his wheelchair to co-author Constance Emerson Crooker, who adds commentary to give context.

"A Remarkable and Truly Honest Book About War: No heroics nor flag-waving, not even much anti-war grandstanding, just a wrenching day-by-miserable-day report from the front. Medic Doc Jackson witnesses war's death and destruction, but the book stands out among war stories for its unembellished truth of dirt, lousy food, contaminated water, snakes, spiders, piss-ants, cruel and ignorant officers, perpetual fear, and the horror of being "expendable." And never enough dry socks! Worried sick about a shaky marriage, endless unpaid bills, a squabbling family, a beloved but failing grandmother, and a baby boy he hardly knows, young Jackson grudgingly serves out his time and comes home pretty much ruined by PTSD and Agent Orange. Doc Jackson's Letters Home is a testament to raw human courage, the will to persist and survive, even to find grim humor in the absurdity of his fate. A remarkable and truly honest book about war."

Rebecca Pepper Sinkler, former editor
in chief, *The New York Times Book Review*

"A Must Read for Pro-Country-Shaping Politicians: When we were in 'Nam, when talking of home, we called it 'the world' because our bizarre existence in what we knew to be a futile war felt like being on another planet. I made my two brothers promise they would not come. The voice of Doc Jackson tells the human cost to our soldiers and the enemy. We came back to society with seen and unseen wounds. This book is a must read for any politician who is thinking of sending young Americans into the carnage of war with the foolish idea of reshaping another country."

John A Wetteland Jr. A Battery, 1/83d ARTY March 1969-
May 1970

"Fascinating letters from a frontline medic with a need to shield his family from war's horrors and dangers while relating daily details of army life. Reveals the weight of war on a twenty two year old married father of a toddler, forced to live in the jungle for weeks without a shower, whilst constantly fearing death. His frustrations with poor leadership in a war against a supposed communist menace to all of Southeast Asia shine through. Although the communists won the war, the consequences of the domino theory never came to pass and today Vietnam is a thriving society."

Peder Bisbjerg, Environmental Engineer
twenty years experience living
and working in Vietnam

"Doc Jackson's letters home were written with incredible honesty and insight that were far beyond his years. His awareness of what he was experiencing was recorded on a daily basis that surpassed great historical writing. It is rare that someone his age at the time of his writing could have such insight. Lying is the most powerful weapon in war, and Doc Jackson's letters home personified his visceral reaction to a war that turned into madness. As Malcolm X once wrote: 'The only thing worse than death is betrayal.' Doc Jackson's legacy of truth is recorded in his letters sent home—history that would become a treasured time capsule."

Mike Hastie, Army Medic Vietnam 1970-71

Doc Jackson's Letters Home:

A Combat Medic's 1968 Letters from Vietnam

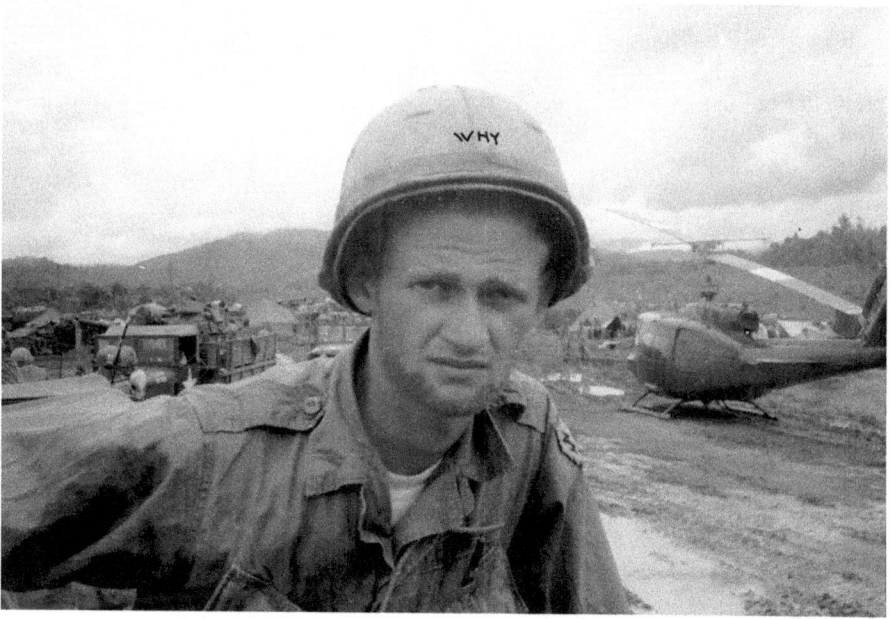

Jerome J. Jackson

and

Constance Emerson Crooker

◇◇◇◇◇

Dedications

To my sons, Blane, Chris, and Tim.

◇

To my father, the Reverend Charles Wescott Crooker, a man of principle who taught that our talents should be held in stewardship and used in the service of others.

About the Authors

Jerome J. Jackson

Oregon born Doc Jerome J. Jackson, 1968 combat medic with the Fourth Infantry Division in Vietnam, awarded Combat Medics' Badge for providing medical aid while under enemy fire, wrote letters home to mother, Hazel Jackson, a schoolteacher and Oklahoma dust bowl exile. Tells wartime recollections to author Crooker.

B.A. in architecture, career as project manager, formal study to become a skilled oil painter. Late in life calling to the ministry led to becoming a Masters of Divinity trained part-time preacher.

Post-traumatic stress disorder casualty, and wheelchair bound victim of Parkinson's disease caused by exposure to the toxic defoliant, Agent Orange. Four times married and divorced. Father to Blane, Chris, and Tim.

Intentionally reclusive life in mountains with chickens, ducks, goats. Son and daughter-in-law, Tim and Mary his caregivers, and his granddaughter Chelsee his perpetual motion comic relief. Rescue dog, Eli the cuddly companion of his lap and bed.

When between wives two and three, Jackson had intermittently been a mercurial paramour of Crooker.

Constance Emerson Crooker

Oregon resident, author, retired lawyer, raised in four of the

New England states, Crooker's Emerson ancestry is in the Ralph Waldo Emerson family tree.

Reed College B.A. in art history. J.D. and career as a bilingual (English/Spanish) lawyer dedicated to giving voice to the voiceless in the face of crushing power.

Author of books and articles on outdoor travel, coping with failing health (www.melanomamama.com), and legal subjects such as gun rights and gun control.

During Chris and Tim's childhoods, caring mother figure during allotted child custody weekends with Jackson, their peripatetic father.

◇◇◇◇◇

Table of Contents

"If his destiny be strange, it is also sublime."
Jules Verne said of Captain Nemo, who, in bitterness, had cut all ties to humanity.

"Yes we burned out the jungles far and wide,
Made sure those red apes had no place left to hide."
Phil Ochs, "Talking Vietnam Blues"

"This involvement is, without a doubt, the most stupid pretense of defending our country that the U.S. will ever see."
Doc Jackson in one of his letters home.

"If I stay here I'll end up serving a prison sentence because I didn't kill somebody."
Doc Jackson, on spending time in the stockade for disobeying an order to board the plane to Vietnam.

"It don't mean nothin', man."
Steve Gardner, Jackson's hometown war buddy.

◇◇◇◇◇

Doc Jackson's Letters Home:

A Combat Medic's 1968 Letters from Vietnam

Private E-1 Jerome Jackson was sent to Vietnam in April, 1968 to serve as a medic with the Fourth Infantry Division of the U.S. Army. He was twenty-two years old. He left behind his twenty-one-year-old wife, Nickie, and their two-year-old toddler, Blane. He also left behind in suburban Beaverton, Oregon his schoolteacher mother, Hazel, beloved grandmother Niny, married sister, Sue, kid sister, Jodi, and Jodi's dog, Josephine, also referred to in his letters as "the rhodent" or "the stupid rhodent." The letters also contain frequent references to Gil, a friend who was supposed to help Jackson get registered for college in order to move his discharge date up. His mother saved all his letters, and shortly after her death in 2014, they were delivered to Doc Jackson, who read them for the first time since he wrote them.

It would be more accurate to say that he had the letters read to him. His eyes could no longer focus on his own small, neat handwriting, and his hand shook when he held the letters. Jerome Jackson, also called Doc, also called Rome, was by then fully disabled from the Parkinson's he developed from his exposure in Vietnam to the toxic defoliant Agent Orange, which the United States dumped indiscriminately on the jungles of Vietnam to clear leaves so that the communist forces would have no place to hide, and to destroy the crops so that rice farmers had to move into the cities, leaving the Viet Cong guerilla fighters with no support in the countryside.

Parkinson's is an incurable, progressive, neurological brain disorder that causes the patient to gradually lose control of muscle movements. When Doc Jackson's letters home came to light, Doc was mostly wheelchair bound, with the ability to take only a few cautious steps. He could still dress and shower himself, eat his own meals, and put himself to bed. Mentally alert, with a decent memory, a sharp wit, and the ability to speak in a Parkinson's-muted voice, he was able to help this collaborator piece together the story of his months as a combat medic in Vietnam.

The Vietnam War was controversial from the start. It was a Southeast Asian civil war with a complicated history of French colonialist control and U.S. intervention, conducted between the north and south in a small country that most Americans couldn't locate on a map. The public was first told that we weren't at war, and that the U.S. had only sent "military advisors" to help the South Vietnamese fend off the communist invaders from North Vietnam. But then, the U.S. troop strength was quietly expanded and our military began to take on combat roles.

Our part in the war (called a "conflict," since Congress never declared war) officially began when, on August 4th, 1964, the USS Maddox, one of two U.S. destroyers stationed in the Gulf of Tonkin, radioed that they had been fired on by North Vietnamese forces, the truth of which historians now question, because the captain of the USS Maddox, immediately after the action, reported that "freak weather effects on radar and overeager sonar men" caused a false report of an attack. Our involvement ended in 1973 following peace talks that were supposed to end the war by reunifying the divided country, however the battle continued between the North and South Vietnamese until Saigon fell to the communists in 1975.

During the bloody ground war, 58,220 U.S. forces were killed, and their names are now memorialized on what has come to be called The Wall, in Washington D.C. The high suicide rate among Vietnam veterans with post-traumatic stress disorder (PTSD) is a national scandal. An estimated two to six million Vietnamese were killed.

By the time Doc Jackson was shipped overseas, the American public had been shocked to learn that nearly 4,000 of our soldiers had been killed in a short period of time in the winter of 1968 during what is now called the TET Offensive, a massive coordinated surprise attack by communist forces on cities and villages throughout South Vietnam. Although the Viet Cong (guerilla fighters) and the NVA (the North Vietnamese Army) — referred to collectively by U.S. forces as "gooks," "dinks," or "Charlie" — were temporarily beaten back from their 1968 offensive, the ferocity and the coordination of the attacks and the size of the northern forces surprised everyone. And the fact that northern forces could hold the major southern city of Hue for one month showed the weakness in the U.S. military's control over South Vietnam, and put into question General Westmoreland's war strategy of search and destroy missions to pile up the enemy body count.

When Doc Jackson's boots hit Vietnamese soil, the U.S. was engaged in a full-scale, bloody ground war in Vietnam. The U.S. public began to suspect that our leaders, who had described the communist forces as too weak for such a massive attack, were at best, wrong, and at worst, incompetent liars. When the arrival home of flag-draped coffins saturated the nightly news, public opinion in this country began to turn against the war. Anti-war protestors soon surfaced throughout the United States. This was not an all-volunteer army. The soldiers in the Vietnam War era were drafted, and many of the young protestors were subject to the draft themselves. They were either frightened of being killed or they were opposed to U.S. military intervention, or both, so many found creative ways, both legal and illegal, to keep themselves out of the Army. This created conflict between the "draft dodgers" or "peace activists" (depending on your point of view), and the soldiers who obeyed the draft law and often got killed or injured in their place. But some soldiers, having seen ludicrous aspects of the war first-hand, sometimes joined with the protestors, and towards the end of the war the organization called Vietnam Veterans Against the War had become strong and effective.

President Lyndon Baines Johnson vigorously defended our presence in Vietnam, and it lost him the next election. (One popular anti-war chant was "Hey, hey, LBJ, how many kids did you kill today?") The country was divided, and many of the soldiers were caught in the middle, between loyalty to buddies and to country, and their own budding awareness of lives lost for no higher purpose.

The conduct of the war itself was controversial even among military men who didn't question the war's purpose. General Westmoreland commanded U.S. military operations in Vietnam until the summer of 1968, and he designed it as a war of attrition, sending units into the dangerous countryside on search and destroy missions with the goal of killing more of them than they killed of us. These were like extended hunting trips in miserable terrain, with armed and hostile human beings as prey. Because it was a defensive war on South Vietnamese soil to protect the southerners from the northern invader, there were no traditional front lines dividing friend from foe. All the troops on both sides milled around in vast stretches of jungle and on rural hillsides, and when they ran into each other, firefights broke out. Vietnamese forces built mazes of hidden underground tunnels where they could disappear, live, and even treat their wounded. U.S. forces would establish bases on cleared hilltops from which they could observe the surrounding area. In many cases, the days were calm, but at night enemy mortars would explode while our soldiers protected themselves in underground bunkers, calling in air support to bomb the coordinates from which the mortars were fired.

Because the hilltops were valued as a good place to gather forces rather than valued as territory won from the enemy, the troops might lose and regain the same hilltop over and over, with no real sense of victory. The only way they could tell if they had "won" any battle was the body count. Success in Vietnam was measured by killing more of them than they killed of you. With the aid of superior air power, the U.S. was successful in slaughtering far more of them, but still more came down from the north to replace them, like the mythical many-headed hydra that couldn't be killed because more heads grew for every head chopped off. Ho Chi Minh's successful scheme was to outlast the U.S., because he understood correctly that we would tire of the war before he would.

Many young soldiers arrived in Vietnam with heads full of John Wayne style heroism for a noble cause. After months in mud and monsoons, with rotting socks, lack of sufficient C-rations and clean water, and the futile taking, losing, and retaking of the same hilltops, the purpose of the war became elusive to many of them. Their purpose became to survive and to help their buddies stay alive until they were "short," with only weeks left before returning to "the world." Cynicism, resentment of military so-called intelligence, and surviving by their wits regardless of regulations became the norm for many.

Doc Jackson fell somewhere between the men who evaded

the draft and the gung ho soldiers. He had voluntarily enlisted at age 19. That meant he had three years to serve, as opposed to draftees who served for two years. The standard time "in country" (meaning in Vietnam) was thirteen months. But Jackson had only six months remaining on his three-year enlistment at the time he was sent overseas.

He was already in uniform with a departure date for Vietnam when he listened to the reasoning of some long-haired anti-war protestors that he met in a bar. They convinced him the war was useless. It was a civil war with the north trying to reunite the divided country and kick out the outside influence of the United States. The United States was propping up a corrupt regime in the south to try to keep communist influence out of Southeast Asia. It made no sense to lose American lives over that. There were some rednecks in the bar who started calling the long haired fellows communists, and Jackson took the side of the long hairs.

When it was time for Jackson to board the plane for Vietnam, he simply stayed in the barracks and didn't board the plane. He told them he was a conscientious objector and wouldn't go kill people. As to this war, that was true. Although he might have agreed that in some circumstances killing during war is necessary, he believed it was wrong in Vietnam.

That resulted in his incarceration in the stockade that was located in the Presidio in San Francisco. He was there for forty-two days, and then faced a court-martial. His parents helped hire a civilian lawyer for his court-martial. He could have been sentenced to a number of years in prison, as were many others who refused to go. The lawyer presented a successful defense based on the fact that the barracks had no windows so Jackson couldn't tell a.m. from p.m. and failed to board the plane because he overslept.

The Army still had to decide what to do with him, so they offered to train him as a medic, explaining that he wouldn't have to kill people or carry a weapon as a medic. He accepted, and got that training stateside.

Another delay resulted from marital difficulties. The Army let him stay to try to work out what looked like a pending divorce. Jackson and his first wife, Nickie, had financial problems over unpaid bills and money owed on a complicated web of loans from Jackson's mother, and the marriage was in serious trouble. By the time Jackson was sent overseas as a medic, he had only six months left to serve on his three-year enlistment.

Once "in country," Doc Jackson was among those observant enough to realize that U.S. decision making could threaten his life and that of his buddies. For example, he wanted to carry his own .45 caliber pistol, because it made for quicker defense in underbrush while carrying a medical aid pack than an unwieldy rifle, but was told that, since only high ranking U.S. officers were permitted sidearms, the distinctive sound of a .45 would cause the enemy to think there were high ranking officers around, and their unit would become a more important target. Of course, letting all the soldiers use such sidearms would have democratized the sound of a .45, but the rule remained firm. So, Doc Jackson had to wrestle with whether or not to disobey that order for his own safety. He goes back and forth in his letters, first asking his family to send a pistol, then telling them not to. In the end, he took a stand for safety. In some of his wartime photos he proudly displays a .45 which had been stripped by another U.S. soldier from the body of a dead enemy, or as they called them, "a dead gook." Its holster bore the star of the northern forces.

People who were not alive then might have difficulty understanding how the U.S. got embroiled in this civil war between the north and south in Vietnam, and why it was tolerated by us, except for the anti-war demonstrators, for so many years. The war was explained to the public first by claiming that we were helping to keep South Vietnam free and democratic by keeping out the invading communists. The war was rationalized by what was called "the domino theory." U.S. citizens were told that the Chinese communists backed the Viet Cong and the NVA, and if we let the northerners seize South Vietnam, the entire Southeast Asian peninsula would fall like dominoes and come under Chinese communist influence. Since the United States had been in a "cold war" against communist countries since shortly after World War II, the war in Vietnam was able to flourish and expand in the soil of the rampant fear of communism already firmly embedded in the minds of U.S. citizens and politicians.

In that era, the U.S. fear of communism was widespread, and it provided a litmus test of patriotism. The young soldiers sent to fight in Vietnam had been the schoolchildren in the 1950s who were taught to "duck and cover" under their school desks to protect themselves in case of a nuclear attack by communists. Many parents of that generation had been caught up in the fear of being blacklisted from employment by the overzealous Senator Eugene McCarthy, who in the early 1950s spearheaded the notorious Senate hearings during which citizens could be subpoenaed before the Senate committee and asked if they were now, or ever had been, members of the communist party. Since the economic depression of the 1930s had highlighted disparities in wealth in the United States, many left-leaning, idealistic young people had played footsy with socialist organizations, and those idealists were easily smeared when the "Red Scare" was at its height.

In the 1960s, nobody could have predicted that the Soviet Union's bastion of communism would collapse under its own weight, nor that Chinese communism would morph into an economically pragmatic system that would open opportunities for world-altering trade with the west. Both communist behemoths were feared and even hated as enemies of our revered capitalistic, democratic way of life. So, propping up the anti-communist regime of South Vietnam against the undue influence of those powerful forces seemed a good idea to many military minds, and many citizens agreed.

Technology has advanced since Vietnam such that a vast, bloody ground war is hardly conceivable in the age of unmanned drones, global positioning systems, and instant worldwide communications, although we have lost too many good foot soldiers in Iraq and Afghanistan. Back then, we had barely begun to lob satellites skyward, and computers that could bounce signals around the world had not been dreamt of. So we sent thousands of our young men to live in wretched conditions and risk their lives in a surreal landscape of mud, monsoons, and endless jungle. The norm was that soldiers would stay in country for terms of thirteen months, but Doc's discharge date from the military was only six months away when he arrived, so his tour lasted half that time. And he found that he could gain an even earlier exit if he could get admitted to college, so he urgently requested that his friends and family help with his college application.

And the boys who huddled in the hooches wrote letters home. They didn't call it snail mail, since it was the only form of mail. The writing paper would get muddy, and cheap ballpoint pens would fail or go missing. The soldiers would lie to their families and tell them things were okay while they suffered horrors by day and terrors by night. Doc Jackson was a combat medic, and medics, although honored and protected by their buddies, had to venture into fields of carnage during dangerous missions. In his letters, Rome spared his family the gory, bloody details, but grisly scenes stayed deeply imprinted in his mind where, for years, they would ambush him in the night in his dreams.

Although he avoided being shot or killed, Doc Jackson returned as injured as any vet, suffering from both post-traumatic stress and from the gradually increasing disabilities imposed by Parkinson's disease which was triggered by exposure to Agent Orange. When asked if there were any medals he should have received but didn't, he said wistfully, "They don't give purple hearts for Parkinson's."

Once back home in "the world," Doc Jackson threw himself into his education, obtaining a Bachelor of Architecture degree at the University of Oregon, but he came just short of becoming a licensed architect. He did work as a draftsman in several architects' firms, however his main career was as a project manager for private and public businesses.

Years later, he contributed his architectural ideas for Oregon's Vietnam Veterans Memorial to the landscape architects in charge of the project. He jotted down his ideas (the papers have been saved), and then he spent time walking with one of them on the hillside that had been set aside for the memorial. While touring the site with the lead design architect, he freely shared his ideas, many of which were in fact incorporated into the final design. On architectural paper, Jackson drew a transition from the road which would include a pause at the beginning, and then another transition to a water feature for reflection. He does not claim this as his idea. It reflected the planning already done at that stage of the project. Then he noted that it should proceed up the hill with the "sense of order and sub-order" seen at Peru's Machu Picchu site. The memorial as built does spiral up the hill after entering at the base of the hill on a straight promenade which ends in a reflecting pool of water. He noted that the memorial should "evoke feelings, as a place to contemplate life and death, and to remember those still unaccounted for," and he jotted down that it should be a "living memorial" to honor all the veterans. He considered whether the names of the dead should appear together at the center, like the wall at Washington, D.C., and whether there should be a "serial approach" of a number of monuments winding up the hill. The memorial as built is called a "Living Memorial," and the site features a series of memorials that appear along the side of a spiral trail, with the names of the war dead in chronological order. Each of these memorials includes information about Oregon's hometown events that the soldiers missed that year, such as a rodeo or a parade. On the 1968 memorial, the year of the disastrous TET offensive, the cluster of names of those killed in action is the largest, and then the names taper down through the remaining years of the war. As designed, the memorial honors the Missing in Action by placing their separate memorial near the top of the hill, where two trees frame distant Mt. Hood.

Jackson considered how the memorial should be incorporated into the surrounding Arboretum and the nearby Forestry Center, including how trails through the woods would join the space, as he was concerned that veterans should feel safe when entering what they would feel was a defensible space, and he considered that some would prefer to enter from near the top of the hill since a hilltop is more defensible than the bottom of the hill. He also considered how any water features would relate to other prominent water features in the city.

The lead designer, landscape architect Lloyd Lindley, recalls meeting with veterans groups to discuss what was important to them, and he took many notes about what they told him, and the resulting memorial, which sweeps across a large hillside near the Portland Zoo, is significant, heart-rending, and veteran sensitive. Lindley does not recall all the specifics of which veterans suggested which ideas, but the ideas written down and saved by

Jackson show that his input must have been well considered and taken into account in the final design.

As an architectural draftsman for other architects, and a project manager for private and public businesses, Jackson was a skilled, intelligent, hard worker, but he often found himself gobsmacked by the nuances of interpersonal relationships. Job losses and four marriages ending in divorce were a legacy of his wartime emotional scars.

For many years, like too many war veterans, his go to response to stress was anger. When he finally realized that anger and pain are two sides of the same coin, his insight opened a crack. He also realized that the toolbox learned during war, such as instant reaction to threat, does not yield the best results in civilian life. Late in life, he graduated from a theological seminary on the GI Bill, and he attributes a calmer, mature acceptance of the horrors of war to help from God. Although he is wheelchair bound for the rest of his life, he is spirit led, and takes solace in the Biblical promise of heaven.

In the end, with the U.S., having withdrawn boots on the ground a couple of years earlier during a process called Vietnamization, Saigon fell to the communists on April 30, 1975, and there was a mad scramble for the safety of helicopter flights to waiting U.S. warships. The domino theory failed to come to pass. Vietnam has settled into a country run by often corrupt bureaucrats, like many small communist countries, but they haven't successfully spread their brand of communist revolution to infect the whole region, as feared by U.S. policy makers. It turned out to be, as Ho Chi Minh had always claimed, a civil war, and a war of independence that successfully repelled colonial control of the country. Ho Chi Minh died in 1969, and never learned the outcome of the war. Vietnam now invites tourism to its shores, its shrines, and its intriguing waterways. Although efficiency and fairness are not the watchwords of their present system, they never became the global threat we feared.

So why revisit that war now through one medic's letters home? Doc Jackson wasn't present for any of the historically remembered battles such as the peak of the TET offensive, or Hamburger Hill. He performed no battlefield heroics other than selflessly rushing into conflict when he heard the call of "Medic!" He was an ordinary private who was ordered to sleep in mud for weeks on end in run-of-the-mill backwaters of Vietnam, covered in leeches, with socks rotting on his feet. That makes his story average, which makes it all the more poignant, because it is the story of what most of our soldiers went through.

Jackson's story reveals what a soldier longed to have sent from home — clean socks, a raincoat that wasn't falling apart, pens and paper on which to write letters home, familiar snacks, and film for his camera. It tells of the burdens on a twenty-two-year-old married father who tries to arrange for payments on their new TV, and to pay on a complicated network of loans from his mother, while trying to mediate disputes between meddling Mom and young wife, all from a bunker thousands of miles away.

And his is an all-too-common story of the aftermath of war. From post -traumatic stress to an array of Agent Orange-caused illnesses, a generation of our men live daily with the damage that the Vietnam war caused them. Many vets suffer the same recurring dream. They dream they find themselves back there, and they are terrified, wondering how they got stuck in Vietnam again. They struggle through marital difficulties, workplace conflicts, and they never quite feel they belong again in "the world" that they had so often longed for. They know their hypersensitivity to threat is dysfunctional in the civilian world, yet they cherish it as the lifesaving trait that kept them from being killed.

This is also the story of an insider's growing skepticism about the decisions of those in power. It reveals Jackson's keen critique of the insanity of the war, and of the mindless U.S. decisions that put their lives at risk. He rails at the stupidity of LBJ ordering a "peace ceasefire" just after the TET offensive. From their bunkers, they could hear the "gooks" at night using the lull to get resupplied from the north, yet they weren't permitted to attack the supply routes. He writes that they could "steal LBJ's pants right off him during one of his useless speeches, and he wouldn't notice." He writes that, if he were there longer, he would join the North "to be on the laughing end of this joke, not its butt."

If we are ever to get past being puppets to fearmongers who pull our strings with bumper sticker rhetoric, convincing us to throw our national resources and the lives of our young people at remote problems which our government has no chance of solving, it is important to look deeply into how power works to control us, and how one bright individual with inside experience gradually began to question authority and to see through institutional lies, if only to save his and his comrades' butts in a life-threatening environment. I say "gradually," because he started off enlisting, and it wasn't until the war was well underway that anti-war protestors convinced him of the war's uselessness. He tried to stay out of Vietnam, even going to jail to keep from participating, but once in Vietnam, he was loyal to those around him, and he even took on dangerous guard duty that he was not required to do (he was a medic who was exempt from such tasks) because he insisted on pulling his weight with the other guys. He easily adopted the dehumanizing jargon of the day, calling the North Vietnamese "gooks," and he still laughs at how one helicopter gunner "un-assed" a cliff beside a waterfall a mile away on the Dak To river, by firing his M80 grenade launcher from on high into the water for fun, and spraying a frightened fellow on the cliff into running to hide, without even knowing if the man was an enemy. "Un-assed a cliff?" one might ask. Scaring the "ass" off the cliff, which is referred to as "un-assing the A.O. (area of operation)."

And he sometimes took pleasure in the death their superior air power could rain on an enemy out to kill them. He describes one fight that, while resulting in a few U.S. deaths, was saved by the air attack of "Puff the Magic Dragon," a sinister looking gunship, an AC-47 plane with enough massive firepower to mow down forests. He sums up the battle in six short words: "Beaucoup dead gooks. Good ol' Puff."

In his letters, at first, Doc Jackson began reluctantly revealing disturbing truths about the grim war conditions to his family, asking them to tell no one, afraid that it would be viewed as a betrayal; but by the end of his tour of duty, he had become a sharp tongued observer of the life-crushing madness that had thrown him, Tweety Bird, Revenewer, Delta Polite, Admiral Dewey, Lanky, Preacher, Teach, Chico, Gardner, Humphrey, Big Head, and all his friends into the pits of hell.

On his return home, there were no hugs at the airport, and no banners thanking him for his service. When he arrived at Fort Lewis in Washington State, expecting his wife and baby to meet him, he waited for hours, for the woman he had so frequently written and had tried so hard to support on his puny paycheck, but she failed to show. She later told him she couldn't come get him because "the baby was asleep." To this day, Doc Jackson cannot bear to watch the television reports showing soldiers returning to the arms of wives and kids who cry and squeal with delight. The marriage to his beloved Nickie, the marriage that helped keep him sane and longing for home, lasted only forty-one more days before he walked out after an argument "over something stupid," never to return. She kept him from seeing his son Blane for eleven years, and only when the boy became an adult, did Blane return into his dad's life. Doc Jackson missed his son's entire childhood.

In 1982, when The Wall with its names of our war dead was to be dedicated in Washington, D.C., Jackson, who lacked resources to fly there, hitchhiked 3,000 miles from Oregon in order to be present at this profoundly moving recognition of the sacrifice of more than 58,000 servicemen and women. While there, he photographed the portion of The Wall that displayed the name "James G. Humphrey," a man in his unit who was killed in an ambush while on patrol. TV cameras picked him out, and his heartfelt comments appeared on our nightly news in Oregon.

When a similar type of memorial was being designed to be built across from the zoo in Oregon's Washington Park, he heeded the call for veterans to submit their ideas to the landscape architects in charge of the project. Doc also joined with vets who sought recognition for wartime sacrifice by fundraising for Oregon's Vietnam Veterans Memorial. He still proudly wears a V.V.O.M.F. baseball cap (Vietnam Veterans of Oregon Memorial Fund). During that time, he emerged from his reclusive existence to march in a Veterans Day parade, and for the first time he heard bystanders calling out, "Thank you for your service." Those long overdue words brought tears to his grizzled eyes.

People who had opposed the war had, for the most part, neglected to honor the young men who, when drafted, had obeyed the law and done as their country commanded. Anti-war protestors were sometimes guilty of confusing the warriors with the policy makers, and some soldiers, on their return to "the world," were said to have been hollered at in airports with the cruel words "Baby killer!" There is some doubt this actually happened, but there were enough reports of our troops killing innocent civilians, such as the famous My Lai massacre of a whole village, that emotions ran high on the subject of the moral culpability of some of our soldiers. But in a war where the goal was to rack up the body count and where you couldn't tell friend from foe in the rural countryside, civilian deaths were an inevitable consequence of U.S. war policy. Nobody thanked them for their service until years later when memorials were finally built and when the Vietnam vets would finally come to march in Veterans Day parades. "March" is a bit of an exaggeration. While World War II and Korean War vets would don parts of old uniforms and line up to march in orderly fashion, the Vietnam vets would show up unshaven, some with railroad bandanas tied as headbands, and with unruly dogs on leashes, and girlfriends and wives tagging along, and they would amble in a disorganized mass whenever they participated in these parades. These men hated regimentation, and weren't about to start marching in lockstep.

Two more boys, Chris and Tim, resulted from a soon-to-fail second marriage, but this time Doc was tenacious about grabbing every minute of visitation allowed him, and he was a dedicated part-time dad. Doc continued from woman to woman, but seemed unable to form lasting love due to emotional distance caused by post-traumatic stress combined with choosing inappropriate matches. When he was teased about his failure to pick compatible women, he was genuinely puzzled, and he replied, "How do you do that?" Lack of ability to function in the social and emotional realm is a hallmark of PTSD. A third marriage to an abusive alcoholic woman ended soon in a third divorce.

A fourth marriage to Virginia, a much kinder, sweeter woman of Native American descent, also brought about a brief divorce, but they returned to each other, remarried, and he stayed to help her through her years of dementia plus her slow death in a nursing home from ovarian cancer complicated by diabetes and chronic obstructive pulmonary disease, at a time when she was unable to help him with his advancing Parkinson's disease. He still wears Virginia's wedding band on his pinkie finger.

He and Virginia had both become devout, evangelical, spirit-led Christians. Doc had first received the baptism of the Holy Spirit during a private session with an anointed deacon of a local church in 1974, and, although he went to daytime services where they taught on the Holy Spirit, he found no friends or fellowship there, and he drifted away until many years later when he felt that God had called him to the ministry. He earned a Master of Divinity degree at George Fox University Evangelical Seminary, and became a weekly preacher to a small but devout congregation in the activity room of a high-rise apartment building. But with his voice practically gone from Parkinson's, he retired from active ministry. He maintains his devout beliefs quietly, at home.

He urges people to read the New Testament book of Ephesians, chapter 2, verse 8, in which appears the promise that God's grace will save us not our own good works. His firm belief that he will meet God in heaven has led him to say, "I'm not afraid to die. These are the things on my mind as I sit and watch my land. I'll never again follow some guy down a jungle trail hunting for Papa-San. I'm developing my spiritual side knowing that I'm led by the Holy Spirit."

Late in life, he studied oil painting, and became proficient at producing large canvases depicting tranquil rural scenes, unmarred by any maleficent human presence, and resonating with his sense of spirituality. Doc Jackson had always craved an uncomplicated life nestled in rural tranquility far from crowds of people, and his accomplished, dreamlike paintings reflect that yearning. When Chris and Tim were young, Jackson bought land in the country and used his architectural drafting skills to design and build a cabin hidden in trees.

Doc's rapid response as a medic remained with him. He's the kind of person you'd want around in a medical emergency. Once, years before Parkinson's slowed him down, this collaborator was riding in a car with him when he spotted an injured bicyclist at the side of the road who had been hit by a car. People had gathered around the cyclist, so it was obvious that help was at hand. Still, Jackson slammed on the brakes, jumped out, ran up the hill pushing aside bystanders, and knelt by the cyclist who lay writhing on the ground. He promptly assessed the person's mental alertness, checked for injuries and bleeding, and kept the person alert until the ambulance arrived, preventing him from going into shock. His ability to take charge almost reflexively was impressive, showing that this was an automatic response.

Now, his son Tim, Tim's wife Mary, and their perpetually dancing eight-year-old daughter Chelsee care for him in his home up a dirt road in remote hills. Tim also works as a freelance handyman for their rural neighbors while Mary assists first son Blane's wife in a real estate appraisal business.

The home is a haven with goats, chickens, ducks, turkeys, and dogs — an expanse of green lawn, ringed by protective, elegant cedars, with no views of neighboring property, and with the continuous soothing rumble of a natural waterfall on his land. He is content to move about his property in his electric wheelchair. He invites no non-family visitors except this collaborator, and he does not request trips away from home. Parkinson's has robbed him of the resilience and stamina needed for the rough and tumble of life in the world beyond his restful haven.

Doc's mother, Hazel, the recipient of these letters home, retired from teaching school to a quiet life in Arizona, and for years she called Jerome every evening between six and seven o'clock, until a fall left her bedridden and in failing health. Jodi, the kid sister in this correspondence, had been Hazel's Arizona caregiver. In the end, the siblings moved Hazel back to Oregon where she lived in a nursing home briefly until her death on May 6, 2014 at age ninety-two. Tim transported Doc in his accessible van to visit Hazel one last time shortly before her death. She is buried next to Doc's beloved grandmother Niny, who is mentioned often in these letters.

Also mentioned often in the letters is a friend at home, Gil, who was supposed to help Jackson get enrolled in college but who stole the registration fee and disappeared. Gil is lucky to be alive.

The nightly phone calls from his mother have ceased, and Doc's last strong tether to "the world" has frayed. Although there are those willing to take him for scenic trips in his accessible van, he is more comfortable at home watching goats trim the blackberries, and cuddling with his small, curly-haired, wistful-eyed rescue dog named Eli, who seldom strays more than a few feet from his wheelchair and who crawls under the covers to sleep beside him at night, providing comic relief as a mystery lump that wiggles around under the covers. Jackson picked out the previously abused dog Eli because "he came with a bad rap sheet," so Doc's outlaw spirit resonated. But Eli is now a well behaved, certified therapy dog who can ride on Jackson's lap into public facilities.

Doc Jackson's wartime story is told here in his own words excerpted from his letters home, with limited corrections of spelling and grammar so that the reader can experience directly the strong voice in these hastily written letters, some of which still appear mud stained. He also reminisced with this collaborator who took his stories down verbatim, so the majority of the book is his voice speaking directly. Occasional commentary is inserted by this collaborator to explain context, but this is the true experience of a twenty-two-year-old medic at war for months in dense, muddy, rainy jungle in a war he regarded as pointless, and in which he knew his own government considered him "expendable."

A word about our collaboration to write this book. In between wives number two and three, he had dallied for a few years off and on with this writing collaborator, who is now back as a frequent visitor with him and his energetic, caring family. As collaborator, I try to be objective, but I admit to having a dog in this fight. I too, like many women baby boomers, am wounded by the war. This same good man was robbed from me years ago by war-induced nightmares and mistrust, and now, after a ceasefire in our own hostilities, by the dreadful decay caused by Parkinson's. Thousands of men were robbed from the women of my generation. This story reveals how the misguided decisions of politicians and military brass who were hungry for a war could wreck an entire generation of talented and resourceful men, and divide and weaken the nation those leaders professed to love so much.

In the process of preparing this book, I had the privilege of sitting for hours beside Jackson's wheelchair while I strained to hear his Parkinson's-muted voice. He opened up with stories he had never revealed to anybody, even in the letters. He didn't tell his Mom the most grisly parts of combat. I see Doc Jackson as a bright, artistic, soft-hearted, soft-spoken, injured bird, and my heart breaks at what they did to him. At first, I was worried that it would trigger worse post-traumatic stress when he focused on this subject, but the opposite has happened. I sit with a notebook or my laptop and listen with rapt attention to his stories, and, for the first time in his life, his truth is heard. It's a rare opportunity to get these stories down before Parkinson's takes his speech, and also because vets often don't reveal the grisly stuff, even to each other. But he's now, reluctantly, because he ferociously guards his privacy, telling the truths the letters bring up, that he kept hidden from his mother and from everyone else for all these years.

As bad as it was for him to deal with death and injuries, he is also haunted by his daily grind of removing leeches from his buddies with the hot end of a cigarette, or treating feet destroyed by tromping in mud for days on end. One of the worst jobs ever: combat medic in Vietnam. As one of America's treasured young men, educated in a fine suburban school to believe in his intellectual capacity and in his worth to society, Jackson was stunned and permanently disillusioned on discovering that his country considered him expendable.

Here are the lyrics to a song I wrote for Jerome just before he drifted away from me thirty years ago. Last year I tracked down this widowed recluse, ensconced in his wheelchair with Eli on his lap, living on his remote farm off a dirt road in hills wooded with majestic cedar trees, whose downward sweeping branches on a foggy day can feel like a frown, but a frown that is mitigated by their majestically sturdy, straight trunks that stand guard with stoic, silent nobility in a protective circle around Jackson, his family, his farm animals, his dogs, and one hell-of-a-mouser cat.

Song to My Vietnam Veteran

It's time to tell you what's been on my mind.
This woman's gonna have her say.
It's time to tell you before it's too late.
Before you turn and run away.

Chorus:
I feel you slippin' out of my arms.
I feel you driftin' away.
I know it ain't your fault
There's things on your mind.
What can I do to make you want to stay?

You're haunted by memories of years gone by.
Memories of a boy at war
Out in the jungle, down in the mud,
Seein' things he never saw before.

You can't hide your anger, you can't hide your pain,
Can't hide when you're crippled inside.
This woman loves you but can't understand
Why you always need to run away and hide.

You were a pawn in history's game
A prisoner of your own country's war.
I'll never know the things that you felt
Sleeping on death's front door.

Doc Jackson's Letters and Stories

Doc Jackson's letters home have been transcribed as written by him, mostly in 1968, without corrections. Each letter is preceded by a short description of the topics he covered. Interspersed in and between the letters are this collaborator's comments that give context to the letters. Also interspersed are Doc Jackson's present day recollections of events as described to his collaborator. These recollections fill in details omitted in the letters home, and include some raw descriptions which he usually toned down in the letters to keep his family from worrying. After his letters come three letters written to Jackson by Tweety Bird, a gunner who remained in Vietnam and who updated Jackson on tragic events after Jackson had returned to "the world."

Jackson's first letter, in December of 1966, was sent after Jackson had served forty-two days in the stockade in the Presidio in San Francisco. He had received his orders to go to Vietnam, and he simply remained in his barracks and refused to board the plane. Jackson explains it this way:

When I was nineteen, I enlisted in the Army, because I wanted to be in the Nike Hercules missile program which I never did. When I got to Fort Bliss, Texas, they pulled my security clearance and sent me to Fort Leonard Wood, Missouri. I was trained for eight weeks in the Army Corps of Engineers. I was at the Oakland Army Base waiting to ship out to Vietnam, and that's where I drew the line and refused to get on the plane. I refused a direct order to board the flight. The order was issued by a Captain.

They had me sit in the hall and wait six to eight hours to talk to the commanding officer. I knew it would go easier if I listed myself as a conscientious objector, so I told them I was a conscientious objector. I told them that my faith in God kept me from killing another human being. He said to me, "I hope your God isn't the same God as my God." But I wasn't faking it as far as Vietnam went. Even though there are some justifiable circumstances for war, I believed this war was wrong, and I didn't want to murder people for nothing.

I went back to the hall to wait, and along came a supply sergeant wearing a .45 caliber pistol, and marched me off to jail. They put me in the Army stockade at the Presidio, San Francisco, California. When I got into the stockade the first guy I ran into told me there was another conscientious objector there. I found him. Hershel D. B. I asked what religious denomination he was, and he said, "I'm not. I'm a Green Beret. I dropped acid (the psychedelic drug LSD), got hung up on my girlfriend's nipple and decided not to go to Vietnam."

They took away my wedding ring and my wallet, and I signed my name across the seal. They took away my khakis and issued me fatigues. They outfitted me for life in the stockade — tooth powder, shaving kit, and a bunk.

The jail was a large rectangular room in a concrete structure that had a cage made of jail bars inside the room. There were about twenty others in the same cage. Mine was the northern most bunk. I could climb up and watch the ships go out under the Golden Gate Bridge. Ninety percent of the others were there for going AWOL. The son of the base chaplain was there for being AWOL, and while inside he got caught with pot in a tooth powder container.

I was on the second floor of a building that looked like the Alamo — Spanish influence. I was assigned a post police job (picking up stuff). It turned out cool — a lawn mowing, landscaping operation. It's one of the first jobs I volunteered for. A general had a house on the north end, near the Golden Gate Bridge. I was in back of a pickup going across the Golden Gate Bridge to Sausalito. I mowed a giant yard of deep grass with a conventional lawnmower — it took hours. When I was half done the M.P. was giving me water. Every day we'd go out and we mowed officers' housing. They had giant daisies and eucalyptus trees. For 42 days I was on post police. I had it down to an art, particularly loading the equipment on the truck. Six or eight guys, two mowers, edger, rakes, shovel.

I became a rock star in the stockade. They came to me for advice. I advised a guy how to go AWOL from Fort Ord — to take a taxi, then buy some civilian clothes outside and blend in. It worked until they found him at home and sent him back to the stockade.

After forty-two days, they sent a couple of captains, lawyers or something. They wanted to make me a deal. They were going to try me on failure to obey a direct order of a field grade officer (major or above) — but the captain had made major afterwards., I contacted my mother and asked for a civilian lawyer. She got Albert E. Gately in San Francisco, and we went to trial. Nickie was standing in the hallway talking to an M.P. It cost Mom $1,500. I was facing probably eight years incarcerated and dishonorable discharge. Hershel had gotten six months and a dishonorable discharge.

At the Army court-martial, even though I had told them that I was a conscientious objector, and wouldn't go over there and kill anybody, the lawyer found a different angle to the defense. He found out that the barracks had no windows, so when I was on the witness stand, he asked me if I could tell from inside whether it was day or night. I couldn't. So he argued that I didn't know if it was day or night, so that's why I missed the plane. That worked, and they dismissed it. They took me back to jail, gave me back my clothes, wallet and ring, and I was discharged from the stockade.

The Major sent a driver and took me to the S.P.D. (Special Processing Detachment) halfway between jail and normal military duties. So I won, but I was still in the Army. The night I was released from the stockade they gave me thirty days leave, and my wife Nik and I were relaxing at a cocktail party at my grandfather's where there was a great view overlooking the San Francisco Bay. Nice contrast from jail.

I worked in a sign shop at the S.P.D. at the Presidio. I worked for Roy Devincenzi. I'd go to install new signs on mailboxes when a new general showed up. So this was happy days.

So I was in limbo for nine months at this S.P.D., which is like a halfway house where you go after being in jail. I wasn't locked up there, and I had a car and could go see my wife. I was scared because I knew that when they ordered me to 'Nam again that I would refuse again, and be faced with a second court-martial. I started thinking about taking off with Nickie and Blane to live in either Australia or Canada so I wouldn't have to go to prison.

Nickie came down and stayed at my grandpa's place in Antioch, California. After quite a few months, orders came down, and I went to Fort Sam Houston, Texas to train as a medic. They had acknowledged that I was a conscientious objector, and had told me I wouldn't have to carry weapons as a medic. Of course, what I didn't know is that when I finally got over there I would be out on patrol in the jungle most of the time, and it would be suicide to go unarmed out there. I ended up carrying an M16 rifle and also an unauthorized .45 pistol that another soldier had taken off a dead gook. As a medic, I needed to be unencumbered when running to aid somebody, so a .45 provided me better safety than the heavy M16. I also packed around lots of machine gun ammo so the gunners would have extra in case they ran out. At that point, I chose to be armed for self-defense.

So I trained in Fort Sam Houston for twelve weeks. From there, I was shipped to Fort Ord, California. I let my hair grow, and I hung out with hippies in Monterrey. I went to a tavern to have a beer, and there were two anti-war hippies there. One redneck was attacking them, saying that they must be commies. I told the redneck there was no reason to be in Vietnam. Those hippies took me home and got me stoned on strong pot.

In the shower one time a First Sergeant came through. He saw my long wet hair and asked me my name, and wrote it down, and a week later I had orders to go to Vietnam, because the son of a bitch didn't like my haircut. I got thirty days leave, and Nickie and I drove up to Fort Lewis, Washington. I talked to somebody to try to avoid going, but I got nowhere.

I filled out paperwork for a hardship deferment. Me and Nickie were fighting, and close to a divorce, and I didn't want to manage the divorce from Vietnam. They gave me a job in a dispensary giving shots. That worked for awhile, but they came up short of medics after TET.

Collaborator's comment: As it turns out, Jackson replaced a medic who was killed during the TET offensive. And later, the medic who replaced Jackson was wounded in action.

The warrant officer threatened me physically to get on the plane. I kissed Nickie goodbye, and made the flight. I didn't want to go back to jail again. But I had stalled long enough that I had only six months left in the Army. Also, it put me in time for fall registration for college. I was in Vietnam five months and seventeen days, with no R&R, one hundred percent in the boonies.

So it was while I was at the S.P.D. that I wrote the letter to my mother and grandmother to tell them how scared I was of going to prison again if I refused orders a second time, and how I planned to flee the country instead.

All this time, Nickie went wherever they sent me, and we lived off base and tried to have a normal marriage, but we always had money problems, right from the start. Because of all our complicated debts, we were on the verge of divorce before I even went over there.

After I got to Vietnam, the arrest and jail records didn't follow me, because those pages were missing from my personnel file. Also anything else that was bad about me. An officer noticed gaps in the dates and asked me where the missing pages were. I just said, "What missing pages? That's the whole record the Army has on me." Of course a guy could conceivably get access to his own personnel file and remove derogatory paperwork, but that could get him in trouble, and I would never admit to having done anything like that.

So in the end, I was sent as a medic to Vietnam in April of 1968, even though I had only six months left on my enlistment in the service. I even got those six months cut a little shorter by enrolling in college. That shaved off a few weeks. So I was in country from then until early September. It was less time than other guys who served there for a year, but it was long enough to wreck my life and give me Parkinson's from Agent Orange exposure.

◇◇◇◇◇

» **Will be reclassified as 1-A-O (conscientious ob-jector who won't kill).**
» **Considers fleeing to Canada or Australia.**

The letter below was written to his mother and grandmother in December 1966 from S.P.D. (Special Processing Detachment) after his court-martial. Each of the following letters throughout the book will also be preceded by such introductory summaries, to guide the reader to the topics in which the reader is most interested.

December 21, 1966
Mom & Niny,

I'm on C.Q. tonight [charge of quarters - somebody's always awake at Army quarters], and I'll be up all night, so I thought I'd write.

I'm getting more nervous every day, so I decided (I think) I should do something like write to Washington D.C. - I got the address in D.C., and I'm positive I'll get an answer. I don't know when I'll get around to writing, but I've got to do something soon before I crack up. This whole thing is so complicated that it's unbelievable. I'll talk to Gately first. [Albert E. Gately, the civilian lawyer who had successfully defended his court martial case.] Maybe he knows of a good sedative. My hands shake so bad sometimes that I can't hold a cup of coffee. Now nobody

33

told me I had an ulcer, but I've described to several people my "condition," and they say it's a "nervous stomach" ... cramps and etc. caused by butterflies and acid, like what causes ulcers. I drink milk as often as I can - and it helps. I'll see a doctor soon. Compoz will work until then.

I don't know exactly what brought on this terrible fear of suddenly getting court-martialed, but I've almost "lived" it a thousand times. I come home at night and I feel like when I was a little kid fondling everything. Except it's not only because it seems like years since I've seen something half-way familiar or "secure," but because it almost seems like it's the last time I'll see or touch something of my own or something secure and familiar.

Once the Army gets me in a court room I won't stand a chance. It was almost a joke before, but this time it will be worse... Last time I'd spent 42 days behind bars studying and cramming my mind full of facts and information so that when the time was right I could fire back every verse in the Bible from memory.

Now it's different. I've lost one thing. That is, that I no longer accept being tried. I'm not behind bars now. I'm free to go as I please, and I can't accept being tried for what I believe ... just for what I am! It's not justice. There is no law that says a man has to live here. I want freedom, not the kind these flag waving hipocrits-? call freedom. I mean mental ... peace of mind. I'll go anywhere to be left alone! Including out of the U.S.A. I don't know. If I stay here I'll end up serving a prison sentence because I didn't kill somebody. Can you picture yourself talking to me through chicken wire at Ft. Leavenworth Kansas, Federal Penitentiary? Me convicted of disobeying an order to become a murderer? Something doesn't add up.

The whole thing hit me and I can't hack it. I'd rather move to Australia. If I had the money and the notice (before I got a trial ... if) I would be gone as soon as I could get on a plane. I could send for Nickie & Blane later.

I just don't know.

I didn't write to Dad. It seems like every time I write I ask for money, and I just can't see how he could keep forking it out. It's getting bad and I just can't push it anymore. He'd loan you money before he would me.

Collaborator's comment: Jackson's parents were bitterly divorced when he was a child.

I really feel bad about it.

And I don't know what to do about that money you put out for the car. I've owed a kid $10 for almost 2 months and I can't pay it. We got $50 refund from insurance but Nickie's dentist had been threatening to sue us for 6 months, so he got that. We're broke.

It's about to drive me nuts.

A retired major called several weeks ago and asked for 2 men to paint for him ... for $! So I volunteered. Now this buddy of mine and I are working nights ... or will be again if I ever get off of these cheap details.

He pays $1.50 an hour, and it's been worth about $28 so far. But that only allowed us to eat meat ... for the rest of the month!

And keep gas in the car and food in Blane. Maybe I can get a store-bought haircut. But if I keep working I'll catch up by July of '67. If I'm not in jail.

Promising, isn't it? At least I'll be white if I don't see "Free, White, & 21."

Nickie's parents went on down to L.A. but we won't be going down. For one thing it costs money, and second, I couldn't make it to L.A. either. I --- everybody - only got Sat., Sun. & Mon. off. Looks like a quiet Christmas.

The only people who got leaves around here were the dam trainees who've been here 2 months at the most. I've been in S.P.D. 3 times as long as they've been in the Army. Actually, I wouldn't know what to do with a leave, but I'll try to get one as soon as I accumulate some.

Must go,

Love Rome & Nickie & B.A. (Blane Addison) (5 1/2 teeth)

Write

Dec. 26 - 66

Just got back to this letter.

Thanks so much for the sweaters! They're beautiful. B.A.'s package hasn't arrived yet. - I think you mentioned another package.

I talked to Gately. I told him I'd been to see the Australian Consulate General...but I don't know how to get a passport and visa. So Canada is my only hope.

Before you scoff this "running", let me tell you what happened.

I met the C.O. - Tower in the hall the other day. He said, "Look for orders real soon ... and don't pack your bags to leave the Army." I asked him to explain that, and he said, "It'll be a classification...not a reassignment."

That means I'll be legal 1-A-O Conscientious Objector and still assigned to the 25th infantry division at Da Nang. - as a con. obj. - but chances are I won't get out of this Viet Nam bit - even if I beat it this time, it'll come up again. And next time they'll "hang me" - says Gately.

> Collaborator's comment: Classification 1-A-O is the category for soldiers who are morally opposed to serving in combat, but they can be assigned to military service that doesn't involve combat or weaponry. Thus the offer was made to Jackson to allow him to train as a medic, since medics are not required to carry weapons.

So I'm not going to chalk up 42 days in jail, and 9 months in S.P.D., ulcers and the shakes, all for a classification of 1-A-O, which won't keep me out of Viet Nam.

I don't know what to do.

This all took place since I wrote the first part of this letter.

It's mostly coincidence, but I didn't start planning to "escape" any too soon. Canada has an extradition law, but I can't go anywhere else on so little money and without a passport etc.

I just have to lay low for 10 years then change my name. In 7 years I'll be legally dead.

It's better than a certain prison term. Help me think it over, but look at it as if you were facing a prison term. Wouldn't you go to Canada?

I want to go to Orcas, Horseshoe, or Friday Harbor - or even up further...into Canadian waters.

Be broad minded and tell me what you think. And remember what stockades are really like...let's all go.

It just all depends on what happens in the next week or so. I'll call if anything big happens, and I'll talk to Gately before I make a move.

We just took a drive down the beach about 40 miles - today is a beautiful sunny day. I wore my sweater too. Mr. Weiss used to have a red one just like it, and I always thought it looked so classy. It is something like rich casual men would wear. That's me. Ha!

Must go.

Do write.

Rome, Nickie & B.A.

◇◇◇◇◇

» **Arrival in country.**
» **Mediating between mother and wife.**

Sat. a.m.

Dear Family,

I arrived at Cam Rahn Bay at 9:45 Friday. My time is 16 or 17 hours ahead of yours there, which is pretty confusing.

It's hot enough here. Only 85 or 90, but it's humid - like a steam-bath.

I'll be here at Cam Rahn Bay for probably 4 days, then I'll go to an outfit. 50/50 it'll be the one I'm assigned to. 50/50 it won't be, too.

Being here isn't half as bad as just getting here. It's sorta desert-like here, a lot like Texas. In fact I still can't believe I'm in Viet Nam. It's just like San Antonio. Sand, no trees, except banana, and hot as could be.

So far, everybody I've talked to says I got robbed having to come here with 186 days left in the Army. I'm "shorter" than 98% of the men who've spent as much as 6 months here!

But after all the fooling around, it's a relief to just be here. It's a little bit like camping considering I walk 4 blocks to an outhouse and they've got very little electricity or running water. And this is supposed to be 2nd best in Nam for "comforts." Wow.

This name tag was hand-done on a sewing machine while I watched. A little Vietnamese guy just sewed it like we'd print it. Thought Jodi would like it - or someone. If Mike Nieheiser would like some, I can have them sewn in 5 min/25¢.

I won't have return address until I get permanently "put," and then I'll let you know what it is. It should only be a week or so.

I'm on a "detail" sitting in a supply room nites. Water cooler and a big fan - it's good "work."

I'm doing fine, probably gaining weight like a horse. I'm always starving! And I must've drank a gallon of water today. I feel good, and rested. And most of all, I feel peace of mind at last.

I think you should know, and believe that Nickie didn't want me here; but here rather than in jail. And being here to judge personally, I agree. I don't think you should blame her, it's up to you. She felt a little discriminated against when we were there. Normal feelings I'm sure, but you have to be careful.

She's twice the wife she ever was, because I put more emphasis on being independent. You've heard about that. That doesn't mean cold war, just privacy and independence. I remember your saying you wouldn't "bother" or "infringe" on this particularly independent marriage, and I really feel good about that. I don't ask you to walk like on thin ice or anything else. Please don't go out of your way in any way, and everything will work out beautifully.

I guess that's why I've never felt better.

The only thing I can ask is if you should see Nickie while I'm here, be careful of how you put things. The end.

It's 5:30 Sat a.m. here. Minus about 17 hours would be your time. Almost 1 a.m. I just ate a huge breakfast and I'm going to sit back and unlax awhile.

Take care and don't worry. I'll write soon and keep you posted.

Tell Jodi a special hi from be-other - I left without a kiss.

Much love, Rome

Collaborator's comment: He signs many of his letters "be-other" or else "beother", the childhood name his little sister Jodi called him before she could pronounce "brother."

Jackson fleshed out the shock of his arrival in country by explaining to this collaborator:

> Polyclang was where I was let off in Vietnam. After jungle warfare training I was dropped off at this airstrip in the middle of nowhere. I was alone. The runway there was made of PSP (pierced steel planking) that could be hooked together, and by laying down a couple hundred of them and running over it with a bulldozer to settle it, you could land a small plane there.
>
> So I was sitting on a runway in the middle of nowhere

with clean clothing. It was weird just sitting on a runway. It was clearly a supply depot. There was already a load that had been dropped off with straps still on top of it. I was just sitting waiting for them to come to pick it up and me with it. When they came, it was a short chopper flight. It was rainy with fog hanging in the trees. We landed on a hilltop, and were met by about ten guys. The hilltop was on or near Mile High, which was a place where a lot of men were killed during TET. I was still standing in the door of the chopper when I got my first look at all the filthy, dirty, muddy faces of our troops. I was dressed in neat, clean clothes. I was shocked. Stunned. It was a rush to see all those filthy guys. I had no idea what I'd gotten myself into.

We heard monkeys at night quite often. My first night in Vietnam we're guarding a hilltop — I'm on a side hill. I'm at a firing position, like a park bench, and we hear a noise in the brush. We heard branches rustling and the sound of footprints on jungle floor. We set off flares. We thought it was gooks, so we set off trip flares and a couple of claymore mines. So we squeezed off the claymores — there was also a bright, pink/red flare burning furiously. Claymore mines have plastique and steel balls. When set off they can cut you in half. It was dangerous because sometimes the gooks would sneak up and turn claymore mines to aim back at us, so when we set them off, we'd be shooting at ourselves.

I was with a squad of about four of us, and we walked into the jungle to see what made the sounds, but I was night blind from the flares and deaf from the claymores.

Then they said "okay, you've got to move. You've given away your position." I crawled up the hill. Then I realized I left my rifle. I had to go back down for it — twenty five feet downhill, at night, by myself, while they laughed at me. I think they knew it was monkeys all along, and they put on a light show for me. I had my heart pounding. I distinguished myself by showing up with no rifle. I never left it again. It scared the shit out of me. I didn't have my right mind about me.

The next morning I woke up to a cloud of piss ants on my eyes, ears, face, and clothes. Piss ants are long and reddish, and they have wings. They must have been hatching. I remember thinking, what kind of a place is this — I can't even breathe without inhaling a piss ant.

I had an air mattress to sleep on. Most of the guys got rid of theirs right away because they were heavy, but I kept mine. When it was time to move out I had my air mattress tied on wrong and my pack came apart — my entrenching tool (folding shovel) fell off too. It happened two or three times until I learned to tie my load right. So the whole company had to wait for me.

I soon got rid of my entrenching tool, because it was heavy and somebody else always had one. I chose to pack machine gun ammo instead so the gunner wouldn't run out.

A company is a little over 100 men. A platoon is 28. A squad is about 4.

» **Pleiku combat training.**
» **Assigned to 4th Infantry Division.**

Monday 6:15 a.m.
April 15th

Dear Family -

I have only a few minutes to write.

I can't remember if I told you or not ... It's pitiful, But I did tell Nik, and I guess I forgot to tell you - that I'm at Pleiku. It's above An Khe - you know, where the 1st Cav. is. So I'm above An Khe, and toward Cambodia. I'm at the headquarters of the 4th Infantry Division - the base camp at Pleiku. I'm starting this a.m. to go through 5 days of combat training - so I'll be here for 8 or 10 days.

I wish I had time to explain, but I just have to rush all the time. I did get a letter to Nik and I feel bad that I couldn't get one to you.

I'll write more this p.m. and you'll get another letter the day after you get this - in great detail -

So help me, I'm fine. No problems except not going where I was supposed to!

I'm with the 4th Infantry instead!

I'll write this eve. Don't worry and take care.

Love, Rome

◇◇◇◇◇

» Combat training with "fake alert" is harassment.

April 15, Monday, p.m.

Dear family,

I'm in a 5-day training program, just a refresher of infantry training.

I'm going to the lines as a combat medic within 10 days. It's not too bad a job, lots of air support now, but the monsoons will decrease that. Monsoons start within the week, or next. Then it's sloppy until Sept.

Would you "shove" my school early out a little? Call Gil, would you? Just ask him how it's coming. Nickie has $5 for him.

I'm just killing time and getting suntanned. And doing "cheap-chores." It's a waste. This whole place is.

I'm fine, but I'm dead tired. Long hot days here.

I'll just keep you posted, there aren't many details to tell.

I'm going to get some sleep.

We're supposed to have a fake alert tonite. Just run outside in our

47

undies and jump in a dusty bunker. Buzz. It's just harassment.

I'll quit for now; don't worry. I'm doing great, for here. Don't panic if one day, or two, you don't get a letter. Time is precious here. I average 2 hours off in 12.

Take care,

Love, Rome

◇◇◇◇◇

» **Trying to stay in the rear as a clerk-typist.**
» **Pleiku "safe" because perimeter so far out, but hears guns every night, and a latrine blown up.**
» **Jackson called in some artillery.**

Wed. eve
April 17th

Hello everyone,

Everything is fine with me. It's not very hot now, the monsoons are close. It's just like the hot part of summer in Portland, if not cooler.

I may have found a break. I ran into a guy from Baker, whose wife works in Portland. We got to talking, and to make a long story short, I got in good with him.

Today I found out that there are lots of medics, but very few clerk typists. So, ... I talked to my friend. The job is almost for sure. I talked to him about an hour ago and he said he'd talked to the Col. day before yesterday about "pulling" men for typist jobs. The Col. said to pull men in non-critical jobs, like medics, and the Col. will push the change-over! This guy said he'd arrange an interview for me tomorrow (Wed. for you) with this Colonel. He said: "Jackson, I shouldn't have any trouble getting you. You'll hear from me tomorrow, go see the Col., and we've got you." I asked him about other orders that might send me to the front. He said "what the Col. says, goes."

It's a relief, to say the least!

This base camp, just outside Pleiku is as safe as downtown Portland. There have been fewer injuries per 10,000 men here, than compared to say Beaverton with 12,000 people.

This place has been attacked 3 times since about August, but the perimeter is so far out that even mortar and rockets barely reach inside camp. The worst damage from 96 rounds of 82 mm mortar and 2.75" rockets, and 3 different attacks was one latrine blown up! And nobody was in it.

Every nite I hear our big guns firing - 105 mm cannons and 8" guns. They reach outside the perimeter well enough. Max. range of 23 miles for a 900 - or is it 1,000 lb. shell! We've got the 4th Aviation Battalion here with fully armed gunships and a 36 hour supply of 200,000 candle power flares - on each helicopter. Charlie won't come near here.

I got to call in some artillery yesterday. I'll tell you about that later.

I like Pleiku actually. I'm in the central highlands, and that accounts for the weather being like it is. It's beautiful if I don't work too hard. It can get hot with very little effort.

Just pray for this desk job!

If ever you're wondering about something, call Gil. He can get info from Nickie.

Take care, pray, and don't worry.

Love, Rome

No time to re-read, so good luck.

◇◇◇◇◇

» **Typist job fell through.**
» **Hopes Gil gets him registered in college.**
» **5 months, 19 1/2 days left; shorter if admitted to college.**

Sat. a.m.
April 20th

Family,

My typist job fell through - it was just timing that caused the opening for a clerk, and timing that put 7 guys in front of me - one has a degree in business or accounting or something.

I got orders last nite for the 1st Brigade of the 35th Infantry, but, it's Headquarters Company of that outfit. That's a "back" assignment. It's probably an aid station (same as a dispensary or clinic) in the rear. Gil could tell you more about it - the word Infantry is misleading here. I could get reassigned from there, but I doubt it. I'll leave this a.m. at 8:30 - it's 7:30 now, so I must hurry.

I'm fine - just a little riled. The back of the Argus [camera] won't close now, and all I did was change film. No bumps - nothing. It's got a rubber band like the old one now. The case isn't sprung, the latch just won't hold. Shut it, it snaps shut, then falls open.

53

Good on film. I left it alone and I'll have it looked at when I get back. It'll work like it is - it'll have to!

Nothing is new and I'm fine and doing well. Looking forward to leaving this hill though. Pray for school. Sure hope Gil did his job and talked to the school. The better he talks the better my chances of coming home like I left.

Take care, and don't worry. Times I can only get out 1 letter. Of course it goes to Nickie. You could call her - on your own; I didn't suggest it - or have Gil call for you. She's got the news.

Be home 5 mo 19 1/2 days. Less if school.

Love Jerome

◇◇◇◇◇

- » **He needs a hunting knife.**
- » **Doc will be on front until Gil achieves early out for college or until Doc is shot or hits a booby trap.**

Monday, April 22

Dear Family,

I'm still in Pleiku, waiting to move to Kontum. I would probably have flown out this morning, but my medical records got lost and I had to go find them.

Kontum is hot and dusty and hilly - with dense jungle. That's where the "TET offensive" hit hardest, there and Dak-to.

I wrote and asked Nickie to call you. I'm in a world of hurt - I need my hunting knife! It should be on Jodi's shelf in her closet, or somewhere with my hunting stuff. If you can't find it, tell her p.d.q. [pretty damned quick] and she'll go buy another one.

I sure hope Gil will talk fast to the people at Portland State. I'll be on the front until he gets my early out. Or until the 10th of Oct, or until I get shot or hit a booby-trap. If he's ever come through with the goods, now's the time. Need I say that the early out could buy my life?

I'll quit for now. Oh, I fixed the camera - it was the latch. It works like new. But it'll probably need a new leather case when I get home, it's hard on a camera out here, but I can only keep it from getting bumps or dropped etc. Dust etc. can't be helped.

Take care and don't worry. I'll keep you posted.

Love, Rome

P.S. New A.P.O. - 96355

◇◇◇◇◇

- » **In Kontum.**
- » **Doc supplied as a medic.**
- » **Criticizes President Johnson for calling a cease-fire that allows NVA to resupply their troops.**
- » **"The most stupid pretense of defending U.S."**
- » **"My only purpose here is to be exterminated."**
- » **Instructs mother re paying loans.**

Wed.
April 24th

Dear family,

I'm still at Kontum - I was supposed to go to Dak-to, but I ended up here. I got here Tues. a.m. and I'll probably leave Thurs. sometime. I'm being given all of the medications and dressings, aid bags and weapons I'll need. I'm getting oriented and supplied like for a safari.

Kontum is like something you'd see in "Bridge on the River Kwai." It's hilly and dense with jungle, and it's hot and dry. They call it the dust bowl, but it won't be for long. It rained yesterday for an hour or so and this place was almost flooded - today is hotter and dustier than ever.

This place is the most comfortable I've seen in Vietnam, even though it's the last stop before the "front." There's a T.V. station in Pleiku, and we get the latest propaganda - some guy named Clifford in the States is doing a lot of talking. Seems like that's all they ever do over there. That damned Johnson [President Lyndon Baines Johnson] and his peace talks - peace hell! We can hear the North Viet convoys moving at night - taking advantage of the stopped bombing to resupply their troops. They've almost tripled their strength and now they have weapons better than ours. They've got automatic rifles, machine guns, mortars, rocket launchers and even tanks!

How could one human being be so dumb! They could steal his pants right in the middle of one of his worthless speeches and he'd never notice. It just amazes me how little effort the North Viet have applied to stalling, and they've just completely hood-winked the U.S.

I could just vomit. Somebody must be able to see it, but nothing is ever done. It makes me think that my only purpose here is to be exterminated - is Johnson on their side?

You may quote me: This involvement is without a doubt the least well-planned, or the most stupid pretense of defending our country that the U.S. will ever see. It's like waging war on skid row in the name of the gypsies.

If I had a year to do here I'd join the North. At least I'd be on the laughing side of this joke, and not the butt.

Probably tomorrow I'll be out in the jungle - sometimes the helicopters don't come in for 2 or 3 days, so don't panic if I can't write for several days. Don't worry, and if there's something you need to know, call Nickie and she'll fill you in. Gil keeps in touch with her - I guess.

Mom, would you be sure to sign that deal from Sears. I've already asked Nickie to give you $20 for the back payments. I'll take care of the guarantee on the T.V. so the picture tube can be fixed for free, but I need an account at Sears now. I can't get it until something is done with the old one. If you take it over I'll pay you back, but I can't make payments on 2 T.V.'s.

I don't know if you follow this or not, but you were behind $17.00 or so. I told Nik to give you $20 to be deducted from the $95 I owe you. Please p.d.q. like sign the account over to your name. It's only $8.50 a month, I'll send $20 every other mo. or something, but this is urgent. Take care, don't worry. I'll write soon.

Love, Rome

P.S. HELP ME GET IN SCHOOL!?

Collaborator's comment: Regarding the medic's supplies that he carried in his pack he recalled:

> When I would go to Pleiku they would give me an M16 and a driver to go pick up drugs for the MASH.

> I carried four or five ampules of morphine in the button pouch on my pants leg. I forgot about them until checking out, and I turned them in unused.

> I carried isopropyl alcohol, "no-shit pills," antibiotics, an-

tihistamine, and a quart of sterile salty water with dextrose in case I had to hang an IV for life giving fluid. When orders came down to carry a second bottle of IV, I didn't. Too much weight. It has to stop somewhere. I heard about some other medic who held the bag of fluid up to start an IV, and it got shot out of his hand!

I also carried bandages that were like a Kotex with ribbons of cloth on all four corners so you could tie them on. I taught the men how to bandage themselves and also how to use the morphine so that I wouldn't have to run to them in case of a firefight. I could toss the supplies to them. Medics that run into combat are dead medics.

They gave me one bar of Ivory soap for washing my hands before minor surgery, but we used it up at a waterfall where we could bathe. We shared the one bar of soap among fifty guys, and used it all up. We set up machine guns at the top of the hill by the waterfall so we could safely wash.

◇◇◇◇◇

» **On a bald topped hill; rotating to the toolies.**
» **How monsoons affect combat.**
» **Doc "cures" a patient.**
» **Steve Gardner has dated one of Doc's old girl-friends.**

Friday eve., May 3rd

Dear family -

Everything is about the same. We moved 5 kilometers South and we're at another bald topped hill. We'll be here 2 or 3 days, just enough time to fix the place up a little and build some bunkers, then we'll probably rotate back out into the toolies for a week or 2. This hill is supposed to be our monsoon headquarters. We'll just keep rotating from here to the toolies and to another landing zone like this called "Dogbone," and back again. If this goes unchanged, and the monsoons last until Sept., I should be home before it gets hot again - and I don't mean weather.

> Collaborator's comment: The monsoons made it difficult both to fight and to get resupplied, so the war tended to cool off in the monsoon months and heat up again in the fall.

Especially if I get the early out for school. If I have to stay until mid-October, I'll see the N.V.A. [North Vietnam Army] get dried-out and resupplied some more (if possible after this peace farce) and all heck will break loose. I just hope I don't have to be here until October. I'm 4 miles from the Cambodian border and I hope the monsoons will affect the gooks. It slows down our resupply and decreases our air power, while L.B.J. [President Lyndon Baines Johnson] gives the gooks time to rest up and hit us so hard we can't think.

I've got a good job. I take care of the second platoon which is 21 men. They call me "Doc" and they take care of me. This is no problem after 6 months in an intensive care unit, but they swear by what I tell them. I pull my share of the load, but I don't have to. I'm not required to pull guard or half of the other things, but I do. About all I do is go where they go and be my own judge of what ails them and how to cure it.

My first "patient" and I were talking, and he's from Portland. [Steve Gardner.] He used to go with Kathee, but he didn't say her name until after he'd talked about her for awhile. That's all I need, but we had quite a talk.

> Collaborator's comment: Jackson had a complicated history with his "slutty high school pal" Kathee, both before and after the war.

I hope everything is going alright with you all. Drop me a line and fill me in.

I'm going to have Nickie pay you the $95. That should make 4 payments on the T.V., and I'll pay it back.

Have you heard anything about my early out for school? Gil will have to do some fancy talking I'm afraid.

Collaborator's comment: Gil, a friend back home, was supposed to help register Jackson for Portland Community College so that he could qualify for an early out from the Army, but Gil disappeared with the registration fee, and went from helpful friend to hated scum in an eye blink.

I'm more worried about all of you than this place. Please take care, all. And Niny, take it easy.

Special hello to Jodi. Tell her beother says hello. Why doesn't Jodi write me a letter or 2?

It's getting dark so I'd better quit for tonite. I'll write as soon as I can.

Don't worry, I'm fine.

This guy from Portland just came up and told me I'm a miracle-worker. I gave him some cold pills and a pain pill like strong aspirin, and made him gargle some salt because he thought he had pneumonia and strep throat. He's "cured." How about that?

Take care.

Much love, Rome

P.S. I put in a "turn-yourself-in pass" that our planes spread over the jungle. It's propaganda, U.S. style. I picked it up just as it landed near our perimeter. [Unfortunately the pass was not found with this letter. Psyop, or Psychological Operations printed up and airdropped "safe conduct" passes to be honored by allied forces encouraging enemy forces in the countryside to turn themselves in.]

◇◇◇◇◇

> » **Writing at night by candle.**
> » **Dirt, torn clothes, lack of food and water.**
> » **Colonel takes place on chopper of badly needed supplies; Doc cries.**
> » **Doc's reluctance to reveal miserable conditions.**
> » **Airlifted from toolies to a place with mail and water.**
> » **Asks to have a revolver sent.**

Thursday Nite
May 9th

Dear Family -

It's nite, and I'm writing by a decrepit candle, so this will be a mess. But it's a letter I guess.

I guess I should explain that I'm with a platoon of 28 men, and I go where they go, being a do-it-yourself doctor. We've been to a number of camps - (Landing Zones.) From these L.Z.'s we go on patrols, several hundred meters outside our perimeter. Sometimes I go. Usually I'm considered V.I.P. and stay on the L.Z. - not really V.I.P., but needed worse on the L.Z. It depends. I'm a line medic, and I go where Δ company's 2nd platoon goes. I'm well armed, and we have more artillery & air support than you'd believe! I got a whole C-4 "Phantom" air-strike on film - 200 yards from this L.Z.! Right here I'm within 5 miles of Cambodia, on the Ho Chi Minh? Trail. Air support does our work, and we haven't heard a peep in the 4 or 5 days we've been here. I'll have pictures and stories when I get home. For now, you've got the details. There is nothing here worth mentioning. My time is spent digging and building a bunker to live in. It's a wet stormy mess at nite, hot during the day. After 10 days, I was able yesterday to shave and brush my teeth. I'm wearing the same clothes and dirt that I left Pleiku with 25 days ago - a month by the time you get this. We're (us medics) trying to build a shower, but we can't get clothes. Mine are torn from vines and rocks, but other than this I'm fine. I'll wash, (in due time, probably in a month or 2), and I have beaucoup medicine for myself & my men to counteract the filth. I don't want you to say a word to anyone. All I can do is ask. To try to "help" or get attention brought on this would be a betrayal to me comparable to giving Jodi to the bitch. It's a personal thing, and it cannot be changed. It's the side of the war you'll never see on Huntley-Brinkley, and even they couldn't help. Keep it to yourselves and I'll explain in detail soon. I'm telling you this with hesitation, but I trust that you'll remain "uninformed." You asked for the truth. I'll try to fill you in.

It's hard to believe, but during the approx. 10 days we were without adequate food (not enough C-rats) - no hot meals, and no water except stagnant pools. The damned Col. came to "see us" a dozen times (inspections etc. He bitched because we were "filthy, unshaven, and smelled bad.") - He took the space on the chopper that would have been food, water, and mail!! After 8 days we were told we were getting hot chow and water and mail, and some beer & pop. Guys were so happy they had tears in their eyes. When the "bird" came in and set down on our L.Z., the Col. got off. Our hot chow was left at L.Z. Polyclang, with our water and mail, not to mention 124 quarts of fresh milk!! I sat down and cried.

We were air-lifted out the a.m. of the 11th day and arrived near the Cambodian border to find mail and water. It's a little better now. Rumor has it that we'll stay here for 3 mo. or so. I hope so. We're well dug in and we're all "plotted" by artillery and air-support. A guy I sent in a few days ago brought back an imperial quart of Seagrams 7. There is an out while I'm here.

I've told you everything I can think of. I didn't leave out much. It sounds like all I did was complain, but it's just news. It's what's going on.

I haven't been able to write at all for several days, so I'll write Nickie a letter.

Please tell Sue and Roger hello, but use discretion about these circumstances. It's just some kind of pride I guess.

I'll take care of myself. Don't worry. I'll keep you posted on the "news." But I'll save the details for when I get home.

I got a kick out of Josephine's getting out. Stupid rhodent. [Refers to Jodi's dog.]

Tell Jodi hello for me.

Take care everyone. Mom you can send a revolver if you can get the post office to go for it. Convince them that because I'm a medic I need it etc. I doubt they'd go for it. And ammo! No chance of mailing it!? Heck, could you? I wish. If so, a .32 or bigger. I won't be shooting rabbits & birds.

I'll write soon.

Love, Rome

Collaborator's comment: In the preceding letter, Doc described himself as a do-it-yourself doctor who goes with his platoon of 28 men wherever they go. This frequently put him on jungle patrols that lasted for days. He doesn't write home about the day-to-day medical services he provided, but, in addition to direct wounds of war, he was forced to deal with pain, severe cold/bronchitis symptoms, jungle rot (a fungus that grows on perpetually wet feet), and whatever arose. He talked to this collaborator about some of his medical duties:

Whenever Delta Polite came back from the rear, he always came back with the clap, and I sent him in for treatment. He also got a toothache, so I gave him the stuff according to directions, but it made him throw up and gag, but his tooth didn't hurt anymore. Polite was a big guy — so big that his pants ripped out in the crotch, so he wore them hanging loose, like a skirt.

Sleeping on the ground, we would all wake up covered with leeches. I removed leeches with a hot cigarette, and they'd back out and fall off, and I'd step on them. I once took fourteen or sixteen leeches off one guy.

A short guy named Davey chopped his own leg with a machete, and I had to stop the bleeding and call the chopper.

There was a guy with malaria. We poured water on him all night for his fever, and a chopper took him out the next day. They wouldn't fly in the dark. In spite of this, most guys wanted to get malaria because it was a temporary ticket to the rear, so none of us took our malaria pills.

A guy threw a can of gasoline on an already burning fire, and it blew up and burned him so badly he got choppered out.

Bamboo itch is a skin rash from walking through thickets of bamboo. I discovered a remedy for bamboo itch. I put isopropyl alcohol on a 2" by 2" gauze pad and rubbed it into the guy's skin.

Lots of guys got bad coughs, and I had pills for that. Also for the trots.

◇◇◇◇◇

» **Rotating medics to rear.**
» **Wasn't paid.**
» **Hill 830 surrounded by gook foxholes, but protected by artillery airstrikes.**
» **The dirt freeway, Ho Chi Minh Trail.**
» **Mother's Day.**
» **Rather be in 'Nam than court-martialed at home.**
» **The heat.**
» **Less B.S. in the field than in "the world."**

Sat & Sun
May 11 & 12th

Dear Family -

Everything is fine, for being here. There's no need to worry. I'm going to Dak-to to rest for a couple of days. We've got 6 medics temporarily, so we take turns going "back." 2 days every 12 is great. I can get clean, and I'll get a change of clothes if I have to steal them. I'll be able to see some people about our supplies and water, and I'll be able to write a longer letter or at least one on clean paper. I need every min. I can get. And I've got 5¢ in my pocket. They wouldn't pay me. They're "saving" it until May 31st.

I'm on Hill 830, if that's of any interest. There are lots of gooks all around us, but they don't bother us. We found 30 new foxholes (there were 20 yesterday) 80 meters outside of our perimeter. Artillery and airstrikes keep them spread out and disorganized. Now watch L.B.J. stop that. It'd be all over! The N.V.A. troops travel safely into "our" territory now because of the "peace talks cease fire." They aren't half as bad as their tanks, rockets and mortars. They've got a "dirt freeway." I think you call it the Ho Chi Minh "trail"?

Today is Mother's Day. I can't be there which is bad enough, but I can't even send a card. But the thought is there. Happy Mother's Day. Niny too. And Father's Day, and ...

We've had a lot of air-strikes all around us. I heard on the radio last nite that it made the news there. We're just west of Dak-to. The air-strikes are between us and Dak-to.

There isn't much more I can tell you. It's just the same old thing.

Give Sue and Roger a hello for me.

I've gotten 5 letters so far. It's a big help. I wish you wouldn't get so flustered about me being here though. I don't want to come home half as bad as everybody there wants me to. It's not all that bad here. I had it much worse at Ft. Leonard Wood! Much worse. I haven't stood outside when it's -8° for 2 or 3 hours yet, and not one person has tried to interrogate me or court martial me for crossing the street by myself. I'd a lot rather be here!

I'm working on setting up a dispensary here. It will be finished and open for business this week. 3 of us will run it. That's about the latest.

I'm getting used to the heat. I've been in Vietnam 1 month to-day. It's 8:30 a.m., & 80° or so. By 2 p.m. it'll be so hot I'll be wet with sweat, without moving. I drink 5 qts. of water a day, with salt tablets. Can you imagine when they don't bring us water!? It's alright on this hill though. We're in one place, so they get us most of what we need. We've been getting one, sometimes 2 hot meals a day. All together I eat better & feel better here than there - like Ord or Lewis - or anywhere in the U.S., except jail. I weigh about 140 - 145 now. There's very little B.S. here in the field. That's the only thing I won't tolerate! It's bad in the rear though, almost as bad as in the world.

Well, I'll quit for now. I want to get a few of my even fewer things together to take to Dak-to.

I'll write as soon as I can.

Mom, by all means, use every trick you know to get me in school!! It means the diff. between being here after the mon-soons, when the gooks get resupplied and dried out and ready to make a stand and fight, or in a classroom. Need I say more?

I'll let you know about the revolver. I may be able to get a .45 here.

I must go. Take care, and try not to worry ... I don't.

Much love, Rome

Hi Jodi. Be good. I'll see you soon. Take care of the beadie-eyed stupid rhodent. OK? Bye for now.

Be-other

- » **Getting mortared in Dak-to.**
- » **Puff the Magic Dragon gunship.**
- » **F-104 Phantom jets drop Napalm; and "glory run" flyover.**
- » **Prop plane, Skyraider, called Snoopy.**
- » **Instructions about sending revolver.**
- » **First shower and clean clothes in 25 days.**
- » **Stealing and shopping for personal supplies for his men in the field.**
- » **Sprained his ankle jumping into a trench.**

Monday
May 13th

Dear Family -

First of all pardon the writing. All I can find to write with is a refill cartridge, but it writes. I went up to the p.x. but it was closed. I'm in Dak-to by the way. The other medic came back out this a.m. so I came in.

I think you'll be interested to know that we got mortared last nite. There were about 25 rounds in about 15 minutes, but none hit very close. The closest was about 100 feet from us, and we were in underground bunkers; all it did was make a lot of noise. Nobody was hurt. In fact we'd go up on top and watch the hills until we saw a flash - their mortars. Then we'd get the location and their grids and all, then we'd duck inside and wait. Eventually we got the info to 2 artillery batteries and they opened up on the gooks' position with 155 mm guns, firing white phosphorous. The mortars quit p.d.q. Our artillery worked around our perimeter all nite just in case somebody tried to get at us. The Air Force came in with an unbelievable plane we call "Puff" the magic dragon. Puff puts out 16,000 rounds per minute, 4 lead bullets, 1 tracer, 4 lead, 1 tracer and so on. When Puff works out he looks like something from an outer space movie with a red death-ray. The tracers come out so fast that it's just one big red streak, from an altitude of 1500 feet to the ground. It literally breathes fire, that's why it's known as "Puff." This firepower knocks down tees, opens tanks like tin cans, and tramples a 200 yard swath of jungle in one pass. "Puff" is our second best friend. Our favorite is the Air Force's F-104 Phantom jet. It carries 1000 lb. bombs of napalm, and when a Phantom hits, it's all over. I sent Nickie a roll of film, 18 of 20 were of a Phantom air-strike, from the first bomb to their customary "glory run" fly-over through colored smoke; red purple and white smoke grenades popped on our landing zone. They came over one at a time at about 600 mph, 50 feet over our heads and tilting their wings to one side then the other to say hi - or you're welcome - because we were standing on top of our bunkers thanking them and yelling like they'd ended the war. For that day they had. As they flew over they went through the smoke, did a complete roll and went straight up. I've never in my life seen anything to match it, nor have I been so glad to have something like the Phantoms on our side. I've got pictures of all of it that you'll have to see to believe. [Unfortunately, all the photos sent to Nickie were lost to Jackson in their divorce.] Incidentally, we do have good air support. We have an old prop. job called a "Skyraider." I don't know which branch owns them, but they carry enough weapons, rockets and bombs to out-duel a battleship. It's slow, so it's deadly accurate. Ask Herb about the Skyraider. We call him "Snoopy."

I guess you'd better not try to send a revolver. There are so many complications that it wouldn't be worth the risk of me not being able to get it home. If the post-office will O.K. it, and customs, fine. Maybe if you took it apart. Hell, send me the barrel in brownies, the rest in cookies, all heavily wrapped in tin foil. That'd foul up x-ray and if I have to move fast to get to someone it could save my life - I can't be dragging an M-16. Over here I've got a choice; M-16 [rifle] or .45 [pistol]. In the long run the M-16 is best. At 600 rounds a minute on a second's notice I need it. But in a fire-fight I need a pistol because I've got aid bags etc. Do what you can. If you send it in parts, send 2 packages together, half a box of ammo in each - or in another, but I'd like to get it assembled as soon as possible. You could mail a letter on the first (May) for instance and another on the second. I'll get one of them ten days before the other. It's a mess.

I think mailing it like that is best unless you can declare it easily. I'll get it home with no problem - as a harmless disassembled souvenir. Mail it. Colt is good, almost best. In another pkg. mail a holster & belt 2" or more wide with "ammo holders" - like a cowboy - ha! Try to keep the pkgs small - around the size of the one the knife came in, but use good packing. Tin foil or ? I know, tell the post office I cracked the barrel on the one I "have" - then mail part by part. Only ammo has to be "sneaked." I'll send a money order in July for it. OK?

I got a shower and complete change of clothes! First time in 25 days. Ick! I really feel great. I sprained my ankle pretty bad this a.m. - jumping a trench! No better place to be than the 1/35 Aid Station here at Dak-to tho, I'm fine.

There really is no news.

Oh. I won't be in the field for all my time. The last 2 mo. will be here. Medics rotate - like I'm doing now. This is a short one. But I'll be "coming in" in July or Aug. That's good - glad I'm a medic for that.

I'm going to get some sleep. I'm tired. I hobbled 100 miles this afternoon begging, borrowing, and literally stealing clothes, towels & sox for "the guys" out there. Tomorrow it's air mattresses and a trip to the p.x. with a $58 shopping list! They'll do the same for me.

Take care and don't worry, again if possible. I'm fine and have a good excuse to sit a lot.

I'll take beaucoup care. I'd sorta like to get home too.

Much love, Rome

Hi Jodi. Good luck in P.E. - I'll give you some pointers - I sprained my fingers and my wrist that way.

Bye for now, Be-other

(P.S. Too late to re-read; good luck!)

◇◇◇◇◇

» **Needs from home: post cards, pens, rain jacket, canned fruit, pudding, juice, film, suntan lotion.**
» **Frustration over mediating between mother and wife who won't speak to each other.**

Tues. May 14th

Dear family,

I was just thinking about that world atlas. Look due north of Dak-to a little ways - 10 or 15 miles. That's where my L.Z. is. If the map is detailed enough you could get a good idea of where I am. It's also 14 kilometers from Cambodia, for reference.

Great idea! When you write put in 4 or 5 regular post cards. I'll drop you one every day! Keep me supplied.

Would you send me the address of Tommy Luke Florists downtown? Thanks.

No brownies yet. Bet the box went by ship if it was bigger than a 2 lb. coffee can.

I bought a good rain jacket w/ hood from a guy for $2, so if you haven't mailed mine yet don't. If you have, it's ok. I'll sell the $2 one for $5 and wear mine.

You should be getting letters from me more regularly now. I'll be able to write daily with no trouble soon.

I asked Nickie to tell all about me if Gil, Sue or anyone asked. I told her you knew she was "first," of course, & that it's her job to be a good spokesman. I told her I'm anxious to work this out, but if she couldn't be a spokesman to let me know. I just don't get it. I also told her you'd call (someone would) if you didn't hear from me for a week or so; 244-5127.

I didn't make any bones about being mad about this crap. You 2 are going to at least speak if it kills me.

I have no needs whatsoever. Small cans of fruit are good, & already-made pudding, already-made juices and etc. are a treat. I'd really like a roll of 35 mm infra-red film for nite pics. if it's practical. Cheap pens are worth a king's ransom out here...look at this wobbly plastic refill I'm using. I have all medical things & lots of Librium, which I've yet to use. I could use some suntan lotion believe it or not. I got a little burned on my back working with my shirt off. Just something cheap. I've got to run to the p.x. now.

◇◇◇◇◇

» **Pointless assignment camping out on Hill 830.**
» **Hasn't heard from wife.**
» **Wants grandmother to work less and go for a ride someplace.**

Thurs. May 16th

Dear Family,

Everything is fine, for being here. I got a letter today postmarked May 6th. I got one yesterday postmarked the 9th. The one took longer because you put Hq & Hq Co. I guess. It's just good to get mail. I'm glad Sue went by the apartment to see Nickie. I didn't expect it, or was it just to return the shorts? I'd like for her to go by there from time to time, and if Nickie is still in town maybe Sue would let me know. I guess something is wrong. I haven't heard, but like you say, no news is good news.

We're still just sitting here on this hill, waiting. I don't know why we're here, we're not guarding anything. I might as well be camped in the back yard. I guess we're here "participating" in the war. They have to do something with us, so they put us here.

Everything here is a joke. Take malaria pills and water purification pills. Nobody I know uses them. I'm no different than anyone else here. I'd love to get malaria but hepatitis is even better. It's an automatic 30 or 40 days of hospital time. Consider which

81

risk is worse. Both can be cured, and it makes the Army mad, but these guys would rather be sick for a week and rest for another month than be here. Every man in Nam feels like I do, (except the lifers) and around 8 out of 10 talk of protest groups they'd like to join when they get back to the world. Many have written to their Congressmen and newspapers telling how it is. I'd write too if I knew exactly who to write to. It'd probably be a waste of time.

I'm tired for no reason. Just lazy I guess, and bored.

Friday - another dull day. It's hot already, and it's only about 10 am. I'm really getting nervous now. I haven't gotten a letter from Nickie for 10 days. Would you call her and see if everything is alright? I don't even know if she's even getting my letters. It's bad.

Absolutely nothing is new. Still sitting here on hill 830 playing camp-out. I guess it's better than walking around out in the jungle.

Tell everyone hello for me. Niny, don't work so hard. It's just not worth it. all I can do is ask, but I want you to take it easy, and sit down and write me a note. If you have to be doing something, I'd rather you'd be writing to me. It's better for you than trying to do all the work around there. It really bothers me. Take care, ok? I know very well that that work can wait; I'll do it if you'll promise you'll take it easy. I also want you to get outside when it's nice, and go somewhere on Sunday, even if it's just a ride to the store. It means a lot to me, so I want you to promise, ok? I'm fine, don't worry.

Much love, Rome

P.S. Tell Jodi a big hi for me, & the rhodent too.

◇◇◇◇◇

» **Appreciation of Gil (before Gil's betrayal).**
» **Eating well and bathing in river with soap.**
» **Heading back to the boonies.**
» **Stuffed on good food.**

Collaborator's comment: This might be pages three & four of a different letter. It starts in the middle of an idea:

I got just about everything I needed, and a good pen. My ankle is better, it's almost back to normal.

Collaborator's comment: The following references to friend Gil refer to a suicide in Gil's family, and Jackson is trying to lend long-distance support.

I wrote Gil a letter this afternoon. I feel bad about his parents, and about his health. He's done so much for me that I can't believe it, and I feel like I could've done more for him, especially now. In all honesty, Gil is the best friend I've got, and I hold him above all others for what he's done. People will always have something bad to say about Gil, or Nickie; I guess being criticized for my own beliefs has taught me to fight for my own kind. God help the man who can criticize Gil to me. Nobody else will be able to help him.

I'd appreciate it if you'd ask Gil to read this page. Would you? I think my appreciation should be brought to light.

The more I think about my appreciation of all Gil has done, and having him as a friend, the more I think about Oakland. Gil outright stood up to fight every time someone crossed me or threatened me. I'm looking for my chance to do something like that for him. I consider Gil to be the same caliber as a brother. Look at how many of my friends have even paid their respects. To the contrary - Don Weiss is getting some special medical techniques for his trouble-making over interest on a loan Nickie and I got in his name. A suppository with a size 8R boot.

The Goodales are very close to Kathee [a high school friend/ girlfriend] & down on Gil. That accounts for not hearing from them.

I'm a little awed at everyone's concern. Give Sue & Roger my best and tell them the latest. I'd like their address, and if you'll explain to Sue that my letters aren't really dirty, they're just soiled, I'll write. Tell iddy biddy dirl Heidi Grit hello from Uncle Rome.

Also give Joanne & family my best, and please thank whoever sharpened my knife. It's beautiful!

I'll be going back to the "boonies" sometime tomorrow.

I went down to the showers awhile ago, but the pump was broken. I ended up skinny-dipping in the river with my soap, but I'm clean.

Everything is fine, I feel good. I ate enough to kill a horse tonite - ham, pineapple & sweet potatoes. Even ice-cream! Some change. I can barely walk.

I'll quit for now. Take care, and try to go somewhere on Sunday or something so Niny can get out of the house. I mean it. Mom, I'll send the $ if you'll take her to town and go shopping for her. Will you, please? I won't settle for excuses. I won't feel right until you do.

Don't worry about me, I'm fine.

Special hello to Jodi, and a special request that Niny take it easy, for me.

Much love, Rome

◇◇◇◇◇

» **Playing Boy Scout on L.Z. Flower Power.**
» **Angry about mother/wife disputes over debts.**

May 23

Mom -

This is just to let you know I'm fine. Nothing is new.

I'm a little - in fact damned mad about the way things are working out bills-wise. I don't know what's going on except I got screwed into paying off all that $319.00 loan when I gave you $180.00 of it to pay back Dick.

That's ok, I'll pay it off. Nickie wouldn't tell me what's going on - after she and I barely got back together, and had no time to cultivate the whole idea, (of being back together), now the trouble starts already.

> Collaborator's comment: This refers to a separation after disputes with his wife over money problems, before Jackson was sent to Vietnam. They had reconciled only shortly before he got sent overseas.

Tell me, if nothing else, what is between you two, and what's going on?

87

This letter is in the strictest confidence. (I only know that Nickie talked to you.) Everything else has fallen thru, been messed up, misunderstood and done wrong. Here I sit helpless and Gil is blabbing lies and twisting things until I can't trust him.

Tell me what went on, what's with you and Nickie and are you fully aware of exactly what you could do to me!

If you two are on speaking terms, I suggest - demand - that you cut Gil out completely. That way I don't have to sit here and referee.

Call her if you want to know anything. Talk and decide between you.

I told Nickie to pay off the $319 loan. That will pay the $95 I owe you, your share of the T.V., and we'll be even.

If I owe you anything else, and I probably do, don't jeopardize my marriage by telling Nickie I owe $30,000,000 to everyone in the world. Just tell me, and I'll take care of it. Bills caused us to break up once. Please don't advertise that I owe anything.

I'll trust your common sense and discretion - and I encourage your talking to her.

It would be a relief if you 2 would be civil (if possible) and keep in touch. It's easier on me.

I've got to get this in the mail so I'll quit for now.

Absolutely nothing is new here. Still playing Boy Scout on this stupid hill.

It's a landing zone - we've named it "L.Z. Flower Power." It's appropriate for this place.

Take care, write soon.

Don't worry, I'm fine.

Much love, Rome

Special hello to Niny & Jodi - must run.

Collaborator's comment: Jackson recalls this about L.Z. Flower Power:

Flower Power was an L.Z. that was mortared every day, day and night for three weeks. I kept telling them that the mortars were coming from a certain position about a city block away. One time when I was out on patrol with Gardner and a couple of other guys I saw fresh dirt where somebody had been digging tunnels. I reported the position from which the mortars were coming, and they finally believed me. Two F4 Phantoms came over us with barrel rolls through our colored smoke — it looked like they were dropping water heaters, the bombs were so big. It was a fantastic and welcome sight. After the F4 Phantoms rearranged the real estate, the mortars stopped. It became like San Francisco with everybody getting high (plenty of potent Asian pot), and nobody getting mortared or blowed up. It brought peace and tranquility to the neighborhood. We were at Flower Power for thirty days. It was a fun loving little city, and we were well supplied.

They left Flower Power for some time, abandoning it to the enemy. Here's what happened when they returned there:

We were at Flower Power about a month, but left it to the enemy. When we got back, one enemy soldier was popping up from tunnels like a mole. Crankcase (Karenka) finally shot him.

◇◇◇◇◇

» **Bombing brings "the max" on nearby trouble spot.**
» **They should let us fight and turn this joke into a war.**
» **Water delivered to this bug-ridden Boy Scout camp.**
» **Not permitted to carry handgun.**

Sunday nite
May 26

Mom, Niny, & Jodi,

Nothing new here. I suppose you've heard about the B-52 air-strikes north-west of Dak-to. They've been bombing for several days just north-west of here, about a mile or so. I don't know what they're bombing, but I like it. We can't hear the explosions very well, but it shakes the ground violently here. It's like an earthquake - those bombs sure bring "the max" on something out there.

Life on this hill is just the same. I've been filling sandbags for recreation - also so the roof won't leak so bad (I guess that's a more likely reason.) They've managed to get us a 400 gallon water trailer every day. It's on the L.Z. by 10 and dry by noon; there are less than 130 men here. I only drink 5 quart canteens

91

a day now. The weather is bearable now because it's rained about an hour or 2 a day for the last 8 - 10 days. We haven't been flooded for quite awhile. Hope our luck holds out. Things are steadily getting better slowly but surely.

I haven't heard about these peace talks, if they ever started talking. They're going to be very decisive, supposedly. If they fall through there is supposed to be a U.S. offensive to make Korea look sick. Rumor has it that they're going to let us fight, and turn this joke into a war, if we can't settle it. Something is bound to happen, but I doubt if anything very bad will happen until August or Sept, and I should be in "the rear" by then. Saved by the monsoons? Pray for rain!

I just checked into this pistol business. It's a big deal over here so I couldn't carry one. It burns me up. I don't know if it's just this outfit or what, but I couldn't keep it. Hope you haven't sent it already. If you've bought one, tell me and I'll pay you for it - I'm going to buy one when I get home anyway to keep around the house. But anyway, don't send it.

Well, I'll quit for now, I've run out of news and information. That's good I guess.

Mom, don't forget to take Niny, and you all just go someplace to get away for awhile. Go for a drive or shopping, or anyplace.

I've asked Nickie to send a few $. What is being done about that loan we got? Tell me what you want to do with it (when do I tell Nickie to start pmnts. or?) Clue me in and I'll take care of it.

Take care, and don't worry about me in this bug-ridden Boy Scout Camp. I'm fine, & bored.

Tell Sue & Roger hello for me.

Much love, Rome

◇◇◇◇◇

» **Send pens, canned food, sox.**
» **Worried about no word from wife.**
» **Slept in a mud puddle.**

Collaborator's comment: This letter of May 28, 1968 is post-marked May 31, and is the first on which Jackson wrote "Doc Jackson" instead of "J. Jackson" in the return address.

Tues. May 28

Dear family -

I'm sitting on a small runway somewhere with this worthless pen - the best I've owned.

I'm fine. We left the place where we got mortared and now I'm in the process of moving, I don't know where. I'll keep you posted.

Please send 2, 3, or 4, 29¢ med point pens! Lindy, Bic - you know, or a good cheap fountain pen. Also, small cans of fruit/ mandarin oranges, peaches, pears - anything, Vienna sausage, sardines, beans & franks - & the like. Remember that anything you send I have to carry on my back. Yes - G.I. sox I'd love. No pistol. I'm getting a .45. Water is scarce, so small cans of juice (pre-made) would be great.

No mail from Nickie since the 20th! Please find out what's wrong!

I'm fine, just dirty. Slept in a mud puddle last nite but now I'm dry - to say the least. No shade, about 120° here!

Must go. I guess we're going to sleep here again tonite, gotta climb back up the hill to the camp. Typical Army - change of plans.

Take care, write, send fruit, juice, anything wet, still no pkg. at all.

Much love, Rome

Hello Niny & Jodi

Be home in 135 days.

◇◇◇◇◇

- » **Send Wash 'n Dry, vitamins, rain jacket; Army rain jacket fell apart.**
- » **Walked 8 kilometer mine sweep.**
- » **Still no word from wife; worries she's run off.**

Wed. May 29th

Dear family -

I'm fine. I found a stream with a bamboo pole sticking out like a water pipe, and I got a number 1 shower. I like the idea of being clean so well that I want you to stick a wash 'n dry or 2 in each letter. And while I'm "ordering," I'd like a bottle of vitamin tablets believe it or not. Something good for a general lack of everything, and that might also give me some energy. This sun just drains me.

I walked 8 kilometers today escorting a convoy of tanks. It was a mine sweep. After we'd reached our destination, and "opened" the road, we got a ride back. That shower sure helped.

It just started raining, but I've got a good hooch (like a pup tent) and it's tied down & weighted with sandbags so it won't blow away like the last one.

It's good to know I made the papers in the world. Ha! I had to fill out a questionnaire when I got to Pleiku, so that's it.

I'd like to know what Nickie is doing and how she is etc. I don't imagine she'd run off but I know something is wrong. Tell me what you can, ok? But only if you'll call her; no Gil as the middle-man contorted stuff, ok?

My Army rain jacket fell apart, so send mine? I've got a G.I. sweater that's ok & very warm so the rain gear is all I need. Thanx. Must go now. Write. Take care all, 'specially Niny.

Much love, Rome

Collaborator's comment: Regarding accompanying the mine-sweeping tank convoy, Jackson says:

> When we walked down a road, two guys walked ahead of tanks with metal detectors. Fifteen men walked behind the tanks on each side of the road. The roads were deforested for 100 feet on both sides by Agent Orange. We were all exposed to it. I also drank water from a creek I wasn't supposed to drink while on patrol in the jungle. It was most likely contaminated, and that may have been how I got exposed to Agent Orange.

◇◇◇◇◇

» **Extreme frustration at mother/wife miscommunications over debts.**
» **Finally received letters from wife.**
» **Gil beginning to cause trouble.**
» **Saw man blown in pieces by an I.E.D. (improvised explosive device).**
» **Considers writing to Oregon's Senator Wayne Morse.**
» **Doc is known as a protestor.**
» **His helmet says "WHY", and "Save lives, not face" around a peace symbol.**
» **Has the trots from bad water.**

Collaborator's comment: The following letter shows the name "Doc Jackson" on the return address.

May 31st

Dear family,

Pardon this ratty paper but it's all I could find.

I got the brownies you sent - postmarked May 20th. The others never came. The brownies were real good - 10 days didn't hurt them a bit. The instant milk was a good idea - with it I can have instant breakfast - as long as you send both. I had a feast last nite.

I can't believe that you and Nickie are speaking. I got about 6 letters from you yesterday and 2 from Nik. Some of the letters were postmarked the 17th. I got them yesterday. The mail is really a mess.

I'd like to clarify what I owe you, but I'd hoped it could wait until I get home. It just complicates things. I told Nickie to go ahead and pay off the loan, and your share of the T.V. As long as it has been brought out, and it shouldn't have, it has to be made clear. I tell Nickie one thing and you tell her something else. That explains her questioning you for 2 hours - and she's still confused - who wouldn't be!

As long as it has to be like this, send her and me an itemized list of everything I owe you.

Every time I assure her that everything will work out for us and we'll soon be out of debt and be able to start a normal life together, at last, I get a letter from her: "I just talked to you mother, and we owe her $7,500,000,000. Why didn't you tell me!?"

Hell, I didn't know either.

I realize that eventually it has to work itself out, but it's bad now.

I don't blame you, and I've told Nickie to tell me everything. I only demand 2 things of her: that she write, and that she tell all, good, bad, or indifferent.

Please help me to clear this up. Send her a "bill" and one to me so she and I can compare notes. All of "my money" that doesn't go into her allotment, will go to pay it off. This is referred to as "my money." 15 days after my payday, a $ order arrives. You'll be paid from this, so will the loan co. and etc... "my" bills. We didn't get back together so she could pay off the debts I accumulated, so I have asked that it be this way. This is another of my "special" (follow to the letter) requests, and as I have told you before, Nickie is following orders that even she might not understand. She is not to be condemned - would you let her know that you understand this and to not question her actions? It's very important.

> Collaborator's comment: When Jackson got home, Nickie had purchased a new "space age" looking couch and planned to buy herself "fake boobs," spending about $900 of their money.

Gil has been a friend, but he only causes trouble. I've told Nik to stay clear of him, and to say nothing. Now that you two talk, there is no need for a middle man. Nickie told me she'd be more than glad to tell you all.

Here is a perfect example of Gil's mouthing off. I'll wring his damned neck. Neither Nickie or myself feel or felt that you are undermining our marriage. I tried to keep you & her apart because it used to be only trouble. Now that you are able to speak to each other, it means a great deal. I eventually want to see you and Nickie like mother/daughter. This is my ultimate goal. Who could stand a mother v. wife feud! It'd be my responsibility to "side" with Nik, & I would. I don't want this. Need I say more.

Lay everything on the line, show all bills I owe - nothing left to be suspicious of. I almost asked that you start peace-talks when

I left, but it was too impossible. You have already passed my highest hopes for "peace" - I feel better. You wouldn't believe the peace of mind I'd feel if you two could actually get along with each other, not depending on Gil to confuse, twist & distort everything. Please keep up the good work. I told Nickie that I had overlooked some $ I owe you. I told her you'd figure it up and let her & me know.

The past things like your sending money, which I asked for, have been ironed out. Better that they be left buried.

It looks like you're doing well at overcoming and previous probs.

A coffee can works great for mailing things. Fast too. I wouldn't use anything else.

HHC is the correct address. (Hq & Hq Co) Same.

I'm interested in the book. I'd like to read the paper-back if it's out yet - send it?

Never mind film - if you haven't gotten it already. I got some B & W for .50¢ and I have some color, that's all I need.

Turn to back of page # 1.

I'm windier than I thought.

I won't say anything to Nickie other than just trying to settle this. It came up, & has to be settled now.

Thank you for paying the bills that came later. Add them on the list of what I owe you - I want it brought even & settled so it quits coming up.

I'm glad you explained the loan to Nickie. I loaned you $190 to pay Dick back, right? Well that's what I thought, & that's what I told Nickie. Does that tell you why she questions you? I told her I owed you money tho & to pay off the loan. It'll settle itself. I just pray for "peace."

The U.S. is stripping its young men of everything. I saw a man blown in two pieces yesterday by an anti-tank mine. I've started shaking talking about it. He had 54 days left here.

> Collaborator's comment: When Doc Jackson wrote home he occasionally mentioned a few deaths in a casual way, as in this letter. He never told the details of real stories, and never talked about them with anybody until these letters came to light and reminded him of events he has had to live with all these years. The man who was blown to pieces has often haunted his dreams.

Jackson told this collaborator that, north of Kontum, Enlisted Man (Echo Mike) Johnson stepped on an I.E.D. (improvised explosive device). The fuse had been set so that the body weight of a man set it off. Jackson reports:

> It rained body parts. I saw a black mushroom cloud, and for fifty yards around, there were clumps of hair with skin that looked like fuzzy strawberries. Somebody yelled, "Medic!" and I had to make this run fifty yards down the hill, ducking and weaving, while expecting to get shot. While I was still twenty-five yards away, I could see a vast

amount of blood. When I got there, the flies had beat me to it. The flies were in his eyes. He was pretty much gone from the rib cage down. The torso had a head, but the arms were gone. His M16 had only a gun barrel and a trigger. All its other parts were missing.

When our guys came out into the open I said to them, "He don't need no medic." I'm standing right where the I.E.D. went off. The guys milling around by where the explosion took place were supposed to stand three feet apart. Chico was walking around picking up pieces of body and saying, "This ain't no cow, man." We didn't have a body bag, so we put the guy's remains in a 50 caliber machine gun cover — a large canvas bag — one torso, and bits of arms and legs.

When the chopper came for the bag they asked if he was American or gook. I said, "American." Johnson was short. He had like only a little while left.

After the chopper took him away, we got on a truck to Pleiku, and we drove right through the congealed puddle of blood. It was sickening to see.

About a year later, I was walking through a dark parking lot at night where I couldn't see where I was stepping. That's the first time it really hit me that I could have been blown up too, by stepping on something I couldn't see. I still get a creepy feeling if I'm walking in grass that's obscuring the dirt. I don't like walking where I can't see what I'm walking on.

Seeing pieces of humans blown apart was not uncommon, even when a soldier hadn't been present at the firefight. These are the kinds of images that haunt a soldier for a lifetime. Jackson recalls:

Once, when I went to take a dump, I saw a blackened leg from the knee down. It was a gook foot, because it was as wide as it was long, so it never had shoes on it. It wasn't cleanly severed. It looked like it had been exploded by a 12 gauge shotgun.

Yes. Now I'll write. God I'll write - Morse you say? [Oregon Senator Wayne Morse, one of only two senators who voted against the Gulf of Tonkin Resolution] His address, p.d.q. please. I may go to jail again, but somebody has to do something.

I haven't felt like this since I was sinking into that mud-hole. I feel that Morse might be able to get me out of the field/fighting at least - but it must be without publicity. It could be very dangerous. I'm known and recognized as a protestor, and I am among friends here - my men feel as I do. The front of my helmet is marked WHY, and on one side is written: "Save lives, not face" (around a peace symbol). This is known as the "International peace symbol." The mark of peaceful protest.

I'm going to start a letter to Morse today and ask for a reply. Maybe he will help.

I ask that Nickie not be left out if this turns into another "Oakland." [Oakland is where Jackson was arrested for failing to follow orders to board the plane to Vietnam.] In fact she will be foremost, of course, as is only right. I'll tell her about this, and because I've done so, she'll be very much with me - but only if she is recognized in her "role." A simple thing, but important.

I'm glad Niny is well. I love her - she's mom too, and I worry about her, and I feel better knowing she's well, and I like getting letters from her. I want more than anything to live up to her hopes of me, and so help me, I will.

It would help if you'd stick in a couple of pieces of paper & envelope. I'm always low on it.

I'm fine. I've had trots - bad water, but much better today. Don't worry, I'll take care.

Well ma, and Niny, a protest is forming. I feel it coming on. Ready; set ...

I'll write every chance. I feel much comforted by everything as it is there. I hope things go well.

Much love, Rome

P.S. Tell Jodi a big hello from Be-other.

$$\Diamond\Diamond\Diamond\Diamond\Diamond$$

- » Four day hike with seventy-five pound pack in rain.
- » Fat-ass major didn't like our landing zone.
- » After three weeks got clean clothes, but wet sox rotted off.
- » Convoy to Kontum
- » Robert F. Kennedy assassinated.
- » More mother/wife mediation.
- » Sister Jodi sends Peanut funnies.
- » Doc prays to get malaria.
- » Letter to Senator Morse.
- » Needs foot powder, sox, Wash 'n Dry, clean hanky.

June 7th

Dear family -

I'm fine, there isn't a lot I can say.

We left the fire-base where we were for 22 days (Flower Power) and moved to another hill. We were there for several days, then they flew us out to another hill out in the remotest part of this area.

We walked for 4 days straight through terrain that is a nitemare with packs on our backs. Mine weighs about 75 lbs. I about died. It rained every day of it and was hot days and cold nites. It was hell. That's an understatement, but I can't begin to tell you in a letter what it was like. I just hope I never have to go through anything like that again.

Collaborator's comment: What Jackson didn't elaborate on about being out on patrol, he reported to this collaborator:

We were in a low-lying area — a flat area, bottomland. Small creeks come together there. The bamboo forest is twenty feet tall. Bamboo roots are so thick you couldn't dig a hole to sleep in, and if you did, the water would fill it up. So we're exposed, with no foxhole, living on C-rations. I happened to have in my backpack two dozen chocolate chip cookies Nickie's sister sent. It was an un-protected area. Leeches too. We lay down to sleep on the ground and took turns pulling guard duty. The ground is all wet. It's getting dark and nowhere to go — we'd just bed down on the ground in the water — watching American satellites when you could see the sky.

We'd get up in the morning and be soaking wet. Clothes stuck to you. By noon you'd be dry if it didn't rain. If it continued to rain, you didn't dry out — you stayed wet. It would chill you at night something terrible. With no rain, you'd steam until dry.

Socks would rot on our feet. We didn't take our boots off in case we had to suddenly move. Raincoats would rot and fall off.

The "wait-a-minute vine" was like a blackberry vine that grew everywhere. It had stickers with a unique hook that snags your clothes and you have to wait a minute to get it off. The hooks never pointed the way you're going, but always against you, so you had to stop and use both hands to get it off you. It would tear a raincoat. It goes right through vinyl.

You never knew who you'd run into out there. Once we were shot at by friendly fire. We were walking knee deep through vetch (a vine with little purple flowers), and an M60 machine gun opened up to my right. I fell on my face and couldn't see where I was going. I was disoriented. So I'd get up and hop like a bunny to see where I was, and then duck down again. So I was definitely shot at. Somebody yelled, "It's friendly!" So the company commander went over and talked to the ARVN (South Vietnamese) soldiers. They were a confused bunch of rookies shooting at us.

You had to be quiet as you moved. Usually we'd be out there ten days to two weeks at most, then they'd find us a hilltop. We'd come up out of the jungle onto a denuded hilltop where we'd get resupplied and get potable water. We weren't supposed to drink the ground water, but I did. That's probably how I got the Agent Orange in me. Going for days with no water — the heat would suck it right out of you in no time.

If you're on a hill with a bunker, you can burn a candle recessed in the wall and throw bushes over the door.

But out on ground patrol we couldn't have fire because it would be seen. The nights were long — seemed like forever.

At night you hear the "fuck you lizard." It sounds like a person with a high pitched voice yelling, "Fuck you." We also heard monkeys rustling in the bushes.

For some reason they decided to get us out, so we cleared an area about 50' square by a bomb crater & called the choppers. They came for us alright, but some fat-ass major didn't like our landing zone. We packed up again and walked about 2 miles straight up to a place where he liked the choppers to land. It was a damn poor and dangerous place, but we were air-lifted out and put back on our hill that we'd started from. Not Flower Power though - the one we went to from there.

So we stayed there over nite and the next a.m. we got clean clothes. It had been 3 weeks, and my socks had been wet for so long they'd fallen off. Just as we got clean clothes on, they told us to pack up again. They put us on a convoy of 30 or 40 trucks, tanks & etc., and we went to Kontum. From there we went to Polyklang - an airstrip by a river. We stayed the nite there and were just about to get a bath - then they told us to pack up again. They put us on choppers and brought us here.

When I first got to the "toolies" I landed on a hill right next to here. So here I am, right where I started.

To answer your question, there are only buildings in Dak-to, Pleiku, Kontum etc., and most are tents. Here we build hooches - two shelter halves snapped together like a pup-tent. If we ever stay which is too seldom (once in 2 mo.) we build bunkers.

I hear R.F.K. is dead. [Contender for democratic presidential nomination, Robert F. Kennedy, brother of assassinated President John F. Kennedy] I wish his assassin were here. I'd fix him right up. I just hope McCarthy can do something. [Eugene McCarthy was also a contender for the democratic presidential nomination. He ran on an anti-war platform.]

I wrote to Morse, a rough outline, but I can't re-copy it - no time. I don't even have time to ans. your letters.

Collaborator's comment: Refers to Oregon's anti-war U.S. Senator Wayne Morse, one of only two congressional opponents of the Gulf of Tonkin Resolution, which authorized the president to take military action in Vietnam without a declaration of war. Morse said, "We can't win in Asia, so I'm not going to go along with this kind of a program in South Vietnam, at least with my vote, that, in my judgment, is going to kill needlessly untold numbers of American boys, and for nothing."

Foot powder will be good, sox also. But if you send a pkg, send only goodies. Sugar I carry, & it gets heavy - I've used most of it. Kool aid I can seldom use - no water. Wash 'n dry & a clean hanky in with a letter would be good. (Old army hankies.)

I don't need much. I'm too busy to need anything. Nickie will send most.

I never did accuse you of undermining anything. It'll work out, but I'm too busy to worry about it, or to explain why Nickie &

I need money. There's a reason and I'll say again it's not just her.

I hope you can stay on good terms, as you have.

Niny, I won't worry about anything except my hide, and I'm careful. For all the good it does in a place like this.

Nickie will pay the $319 loan. I've told her to so it will only cause confusion to try to yourself. I realized that I owed you money so it'll be taken care of. I just hope I don't hear any more about it.

Tell Jodi I like Peanuts funnies, and I'm glad she's feeling better. I had the same thing I guess. I'd prayed I had malaria or ?

I must go. Take care and write. I'll take care of myself. I'll write as soon as I can.

Love, Rome

P.S. Who is to pay the $46.50 dr. bill from when I was home? Nik has it...

◇◇◇◇◇

» **Sitting on a hill.**
» **Wishes for malaria or broken bone so he'll be sent to a safe area.**
» **Hates being expendable.**
» **No one wants to fight except a pro-Nam lifer, a lieutenant nicknamed Doofus.**
» **Little water, even to drink.**
» **Needs cigarettes.**
» **Sister Jodi sends Cracker Jacks.**

Collaborator's comment: The following letter, written on lined notebook paper on June 9, 1968, still shows spots of mud in 2014, and is brown with dirt. He had found the paper in a trash pile.

June 9
Pardon the dirt again. Very little water even to drink.

Dear family -

Still nothing new, which is good. I'm playing like a Boy Scout again, sitting on this hill camping. But it sure beats walking.

We've had very little water - none to wash with. So as usual, pardon the dirt.

I'm going to apply myself to getting out of the field. It's nerve-wracking. The shorter I get the jumpier I get.

Several co.'s have had contact in this area. In fact, we're on this hill as a reactionary force - or just re-enforcements for anyone who hits trouble. We've been lucky so far, but it's just a matter of time until we move - elsewhere or to fight. Oh how I'd love to get malaria! It's "serious" to you. It's common to us, & very curable & trivial - but it's good for 30 to 60 days in a safe area. I haven't taken a malaria pill since April - & I've been eaten alive by mosquitoes...but no malaria. I'll figure out something, if it's to break a leg. This is no place to be.

I came over here to pacify the damned Army. But it's quite different now. Any ideas? No dreams or nerves. Something "tangible."

I guess I'll give up the idea of writing to Morse [Oregon Senator Wayne Morse]. It couldn't do any good. I'll tell them I want out of the field if I ever get "in" again. I get fighting mad just thinking about being called "expendable" - but there's no one here to fight. They all agree, except one Lt. we've named "Doofus," because he's rather "ingnernt" & naive, & pro-Nam. Damned lifer.

Talk never does any good. I'm thinking "would I or wouldn't I" about a simple fracture of the left forearm - 4 months in Cam Ranh Bay or Japan. I'd love it, but it's easier said than done.

I'll figure out something.

Lovely paper, eh? I found it in the trash pile - but it's cleaner than what I had.

Stick a couple packs of Marlboro Green in the next pkg, ok? No more sugar or Kool aid from now on - I'm well supplied.

I just found out it costs $12.70 to get this film from your camera developed! I'm sending it back first chance I get. That's outrageous. I've sent 3 rolls to Nickie & have one in the camera half-used. That's $50.00 for a few pictures. Wow!

Thanks Jodi for the Cracker Jacks. They're a real rare thing here. I doubt if they'll last long.

I'll quit for now & write as soon as I can. I'm just fine, but that's bad in a way. I'll take care & be careful. You take care too, & write. The mail is coming through now.

Much love, Rome

P.S. Special hello to Niny & Jodi. Glad you've been getting out & around - enjoy the yard, but keep it "fun," not work, ok? Wish I could help with it - & enjoy it too. Keep writing.

Collaborator's comment: Here's an example of Dufus and his ignorance:

> Dufus killed a white monkey with a tail. The monkey screamed like a person when he shot it. He came back with the tail wrapped around his helmet. By killing that monkey he exposed his and our position.

This kind of reckless, life-threatening behavior by commanding officers sometimes got them "fragged" with a grenade by their own men. This collaborator knows another Vietnam veteran who was offered several thousand dollars by the men in his unit to frag one of their commanders.

» Appreciates clean paper brought by a guy Doc sent in with a sprained ankle.
» Finally got water after not brushing teeth since May 1, but only because they have to clean up for a bigwig. ("The more he thinks we're clean, the dirtier we stay.")
» General Westmoreland, architect of the tactic of search and destroy missions to increase enemy body count, leaves Vietnam.
» The clean paper gets dirty before it is sent.
» Casual mention of deaths and injuries with air support doing most of the shooting.

June 10

Dear family -

First I want you to notice the nice clean paper. I'll have it filthy in no time I'm sure. I'd like for you to send some like this if you can. It's great writing on clean stationery.

A big-wig is supposed to come out today, so they got us some water to wash with. I brushed my teeth for the first time since the first of May, shaved, and half washed up. One of the guys I sent in with a sprained ankle brought me this paper, and found a radio. We hooked the radio to a big battery out of an army commo pack and we've got "Dr. Zhivago" playing. Quite a day.

I've sorta lost track, but I show 121 days left here. I'll be discharged in Cam Rahn Bay and finish up the small details at Ft. Lewis.

Rumor has it that if this big-wig likes our hill, we'll be here for up to a month. This I'd like. I should be taken out of the field in another 2 or 3 months, so the longer I can stay in one place, the better.

I get a kick out of Jodi's letters - I'm glad she writes.

I'll bet the yard is beautiful - it's hard to imagine it being spring there. I guess this is winter - it's violent whatever it is. Boiling hot or pouring rain.

I hear on the radio Gen. Westmoreland leaves today. I suppose things will get even worse now. One lifer is as bad as the next.

Collaborator's comment: Until this time in 1968, General William Westmoreland had been head of the United States Military Assistance Command in Vietnam. He had pursued a policy of attrition, with the goal of killing so many of the communist forces that they would have to surrender. When the northern forces surprised everyone with their vigor, their organization, and their sheer numbers during the winter 1968 TET offensive, President Lyndon Johnson lost faith in Westmoreland's war of attrition, and replaced him with Gen. Creighton Abrams, who emphasized strengthening South Vietnamese forces while shifting U.S. forces to more defensive roles protecting populated areas. Westmoreland insisted in his memoirs that, if he had been allowed to continue his policy, Vietnam would not have fallen to the communists

No news. Everything is quiet today. Several Co.'s have seen action in this area, but nothing drastic. They killed 4 gooks yesterday in the valley in front of us. One G.I. killed, 3 wounded in another fight. Gunships do all the shooting once contact is made.

I'm fine. Particularly so today I guess. A little cleaner anyway.

I'll keep you posted, don't worry. Tell Sue & Roger & Heidi hi for me. Niny, take care and keep writing, ok?

Bye for now.

Much love, Rome

P.S. I was right - it did turn out filthy. Oh well. There's no way to keep anything clean, living in dirt. Maddening how they get us water to wash with as well as enough to drink because of a big wig, but how about the rest of the time! Typical two-faced Army. The more he thinks we're clean, the dirtier we stay.

Collaborator's comment: The previous letter shows mud stains and grime from forty-six years ago.

◇◇◇◇◇

» **Doc mashed his finger with a machete handle.**
» **Receives from home juice, fruit, kool-aid, sugar, socks, film, foot powder, vitamins, instant breakfast.**
» **Wants sent Sea & Ski, beef jerky, Hostess cup cakes, rain jacket.**
» **Details how hill is secured. Describes his bunker.**
» **"Beaucoup dead gooks. Good ol' Puff." [Puff the Magic Dragon gunship]**
» **Ingenious pudding discovery.**
» **117 days remaining.**

June 13th

Dear family -

First let me explain that I smashed my finger with the handle of a machete and it's very painful so I don't write rite, right?

I got 3 pkgs. yesterday and one just now. Yesterday was much juice, fruit, kool-aid, sugar, socks & film. I don't like for you to send nice socks because it's such a waste. They are a wonderful thing to have though!! Today I got foot powder, vitamins & instant breakfast. Wow. I don't need anything. I can't carry surplus. The vitamins won't last long, so I could use more, but for $ I'll give Nickie the name and have her send some. I could use more Sea & Ski in awhile - those small tubes are perfect. I really can't think of anything I need except beef jerky! and of course juice & fruit, occasionally. The jerky is delicious out here 'cuz there are no spices etc. at all. Just C-Rations. Some Hostess cup-cakes would be good, but smashed. Just the same, if you don't pack them with anything heavy, they'd be fine.

We've moved again. No hill number or anything as yet. This is a good hill, nearly un-attackable. You wouldn't believe the wire rolls (barbed) and booby-traps around our perimeter. Including White Phosphorous, Napalm, & mines, besides mortar shells set with instant-fuzed booby-traps. It's quite a secure feeling.

I'm due to go "rest" for awhile again, as before. Any day now. Can't wait for a shower.

I'm fine as could be. No complaints above normal misery.

We're to be on this hill for 1 week, then the entire 3rd brigade goes near Dak-To for a "good" while. No other news available as yet, other than the brigade move will be for "rest." The gooks are rapidly retreating (past us) into Cambodia. There were several small harassment ground attacks along this ridge-line last nite, but small co.'s of gooks. Puff tore them to pieces - not a G.I. wounded! Beaucoup dead gooks. Good ol' Puff.

> Collaborator's comment: Puff the Magic Dragon is the formidable gunship that rains down streams of fire described in a previous letter.

I sure hope you send the rain jacket (civilian) I used to take fishing. The "slicker," green, with the hood, zipper at the neck. Like a duck-hunting rain jacket.

I'm occupying a one-man bunker. It's a lot like a "berth" with a small tee-pee built over the entrance. 6 inch log rafters, well sandbagged. It's quaint, & dry, which counts. An ammo box hung on the wall with the lid flopped down makes a storage cabinet & writing table. Ingenious. I discovered that by crushing C-ration cookies in C-rat. hot chocolate, heat it again: instant pudding! It's not worth a damn but it's ingenious.

My finger is about to give out so I'll quit for awhile.

I'll keep you posted.

I'm fine, so don't worry. 117 days left.

Take care.

Much love, Rome

Special hello to Jodi and Niny. Take care both, Josephine too.

◇◇◇◇◇

» Can't write well due to smashed finger.

June 14

Dear Family -

Just a note to let you know I'm fine.

I can't write like this but I have to because of my finger.

> Collaborator's comment: The handwriting is larger and more loopy. Jackson had smashed his finger with a machete the day before.

I should be going to Dak-To this eve or in the morning, so I'll write from there. Still nothing new - just sitting on this hill now.

I drew up these dumb little cartoons because they're just too true. I may do them better sometime - no time now, so I just sketched them.

> Collaborator's comment: cartoons do not appear with these letters.

Tell Sue and Roger & Heidi hello for me. Niny, you take care - I'll do the same. Jodi, be good, write cuz I like to hear from all of you.

I'm fine, so don't worry. It's about time to eat - I guess we're getting a hot meal tonite.

Take care, all.

I'll write from Dak-To.

Much love, Rome

◇◇◇◇◇

- » **Receives infrared film.**
- » **On the move again.**
- » **Photos of indigenous Montagnards who live half clad.**
- » **Living from Army supplies, not the local economy.**
- » **Plans for three day R & R.**
- » **More stress over mother/wife conflict.**
- » **Feels detached from home.**
- » **Great concern for grandmother.**
- » **With heavily booby trapped perimeter, guard duty seems pointless.**
- » **116 days remaining.**

Collaborator's comment: Undated, but mentions healing finger, so probably written shortly after June 14 letter.

Dear Family -

The infrared film is sure great. I didn't realize until I got it that there are so many uses for it! I was confused when I got it because the enclosed info talked about blue filters & numbers and all sorts of attachments and things. I sure hope it'll work as is. I use it in absolute dark - like infrared.

I feel bad that I haven't been able to write more. We've been moving all the time, and for about 8 or 10 days we were wet and unsettled constantly, and when there was time to write, it was dark, or there was no shelter, or something. But rumor has it now that we'll finally be getting our long-needed annual "monsoon rest." I don't really care what we do, just so we're not hiking around 5 miles a day and living out in the jungle.

Collaborator's comment: Fighting would taper off during summer monsoons, because moving through wet terrain was too difficult for either side.

At least there's a hill-top fire-base, and I hope we keep occupying fire-bases. There are no cities anywhere. I guess you could best picture this whole area like Oregon in the early 1700's. Every 50 - 75 miles you will find a small shanty-town like Dak-To or one like Kontum (which resembles old Dodge City.) There are tribes of Montagnard Indians who live in these central highlands. They live as Africans - half-clad or nude, stone-age and all.

You may find this hard to believe, but I sent Nickie a roll of film - 1/2 of which I used as our convoy passed one of their villages; half of their village turned out to watch. There are no towns to go to, and they're off-limits anyway. The M.P.'s have a monopoly on their beer & Cokes, strawberry wine & etc. They always arrange it like that.

We live from Army and their supplies - no local economy at all.

They brought us clean clothes today - I got a pair of socks and a shirt. They go fast.

I'll be getting a regular 3 day R&R in Vietnam somewhere, and

I'll put in for Vung Tau or Cam Ranh Bay - both nice places. They have water skiing at C.R. Bay. So if there's anything you want let me know in about 60 days and I'll get it for you - if I can.

There still seems to be a cold war going on with Nickie. Every once in awhile she'll come up with something - war-like I guess. There was a matter of her preparing an article for the Sunday paper about me being here. She saw that one, blamed you and said she'd burned the one she had prepared. I told her the Army ran it and of course, if there was anything to do with me, you'd let her do it. I don't get it. Seems Gil told her you and I were sending tapes back & forth too. Typical Gil. I feel sorry for him, but I'm on the verge of beating him for his tales.

I told Nik to just stay away from you completely if it upset her - I can't referee. I guess she'll be peaceable on the phone; but inside she's seething. Jealousy is the only reason, and I can't do anything about it. So let's just let it ride as is. I'll be able to do something when I get home. For now I don't let it bother me because I don't have the time or energy.

I trust that everything is well there. I've been getting mail real well, but they just haven't brought much to us. I did get the foot-powder etc. tho.

I don't need anything now, and I'm quite "well off" for here.

I'm fine I guess, so don't worry. As long as I'm on a hill I'm "safe," and usually pretty rested, fed, watered etc.

I suppose things go on there in a normal way, but I'm so far de-tached that it seems strange.

Mom: I can't think of any reason to worry, but I do, in a way. I keep thinking of Niny plodding up and down stairs and sitting around that empty house all day alone - it gets on my nerves. I wish I could be there to do something, even if it's no good! I seriously want Niny to go as much as she can, wherever she wants, as often as she wants. I guess that's all I need. Arrange it, ok? Niny probably doesn't realize what she means to me, and I worry about that too. I wish I could send something nice - or do something thoughtful, but there's no way. I'll take care of that when I get home, if you'll take care of my requests until then. Is it a deal? It's all I need here - everything else can be obtained one way or another, except Niny.

I suppose Jodi is all ready going strong on summer vacation. I remember when... Tell her to take care, especially on that super-bike, big brother can't be around to watch out for her. Or Josephine for that matter! Stupid Rhodent!

I'm going to get some sleep before I have to go on guard. It's silly. I sit outside my bunker and look at the barbed wire for an hour. Nothing could even get near it without being blown away it's so booby-trapped on the outside perimeter, but I guess it's wiser.

I'll quit for now. Keep the fires burning and all.

116 days!

Take care, ya'll write.

Love, Rome

P.S. I seldom take time to read my letters, so good luck. I also hope you can read this weird writing - my finger is healing well, so maybe in a week or so I'll be able to write again - right.

Collaborator's comment: Jackson mentioned beer parties in the previous letter. Once when his platoon had returned from the boonies to stay at a busy MASH, a helicopter delivered a pallet of beer for them. Jackson says:

> We come back from the shower and our allotment of beer is gone, so we send out a couple of men to scout. The guys who took it are in an above ground bunker with not much headroom — it's a low, sandbag bunker. You had to get on hands and knees to get in it. So I'm talking to a hole in the sandbags from ground up to knee high. I never did see the guys in there. I told them, "I'm Doc Jackson and I'm here to get my beer back." Silence. So I said, "I've got a grenade here, and I've been in the bush for a couple of months. It doesn't matter to me one way or the other. Give me back the beer or I'll roll the grenade in there." The beer started getting handed up through the hole in the sandbags.

He also mentioned the indigenous Montagnards. He reports:

> We liked the Montagnards and gave them candy and meds when we passed through their villages. The Montagnards wouldn't fight, because they believed that if they died outside their village they wouldn't go to heaven. Their chief had a gash from a plow on his lower right leg that I treated. He made me a seven-foot bow, but I had to leave it behind because I couldn't get it on the plane home.

$\diamond\diamond\diamond\diamond\diamond$

- » **Looks forward to resting and swimming in the rear at L.Z. Mickey Mouse.**
- » **Platoon goes "hunting" on ambush patrol while Jackson catches "the first thing smoking" to the rear.**
- » **Describes building a sandbag hooch.**
- » **Boredom: Notices passage of time only because clothes smell worse.**
- » **Wild cocoa parties.**
- » **Received sox, pens, instant milk, cookies.**
- » **Finger healing.**
- » **Tells them not to work so hard painting the house.**
- » **Thanks Jodi for funnies, Sue for sending a joke.**

Monday, June 17th, p.m.

Dear family -

You've asked several times about my moving. We're due to leave this hill in 2 or 3 days, as soon as our co. commander gets back from R&R in Hawaii, and go to L.Z. Mickey Mouse - which is Kontum!! It's a beautifully disorganized base camp - the rear. It's where our supplies come from etc. We're scheduled to be there thruout the monsoons - which are "barely" here. I wish they'd hit hard; they come & go, an hour or 2 a day, sometimes all nite. But still, we're going to get a "rest." There's a river between Kontum and "Mickey Mouse," and it's shallow and wide - daily baths, swimming, beach beer-parties, etc. The stay is "indefinite," could be for 60 days or more. But maybe for only a week... nobody knows yet; it's up to enemy movement etc. Regardless of where I go, my address will be the same. They'll find me.

Tomorrow our platoon is going on an "ambush patrol" - hunting is a better word. A gook came to our "fence" last nite, got as close as he could, and planted a booby-trapped grenade. We heard him and threw a grenade. He got away, and this a.m. we destroyed his handiwork. So, bright and early this platoon (22 men) is going hunting. I'm going to the rear, Mickey Mouse, for my 2 day rest which is now "due." I was supposed to go 3 days ago, but other medics kept being called in, leaving a shortage of medics, requiring me to stay. Now, in the nick of time, I'm catching "the first thing smoking" and going in. What luck.

As for my hooch or pup-tent, it takes hours on end to dig a hole big enough to "live" in, then comes logs for "beams," then the job of filling sandbags, 100 plus to start, and several hundred more to finish the roof etc. The last one took 2 days - record.

Collaborator's comment: They have to be two to three feet thick to absorb the energy of a mortar explosion, so that's why they require so many sandbags. There are nooks and crannies between the sandbags, and one night Gardner awoke screaming, thinking he'd been attacked. A rat had fallen on his chest.

So when I get a chance to sleep, I "crash" anywhere. Then, if we're so fortunate as to be in one place for a week or more, I start a bunker. For short-notice there's a hole someplace, for emergencies.

Collaborator's comment: Sleeping in a hole keeps you from being cut to shreds if an explosion goes off near you.

I'm feeling fine. The only problem is boredom and monotony. It really gets to a person after awhile. Time doesn't pass in hours and days etc. You find out it's Sunday, you eat and go to bed, get up for guard a bunch of times and get a letter or 2 and someone tells you it's Friday. It's like pouring your life down a mole-hole. All you can show for it is no cigarettes because you realize you've been chain smoking, and your clothes smell worse. How else could you know time passes?

I've been getting mail - when they bring it. I got socks and pens today. I'm going to save the socks. I'll get a change (or 5 or 6) in Kontum tomorrow, and I'm going to keep these in my pack. I'll need them if we leave Mickey Mouse. The pens were a lifesaver too. Just about everyone here passes around goodies - it's the rule. I used the instant milk in 3 wild cocoa parties we had. We got water and we couldn't resist. We raided all the c rats, got out the 4 cocoa mixes in each case and made a big coffee can full. I'm well supplied with instant breakfast because it's best with real milk - which is rare. I use a pkg every 3 or 4 days with inst. milk.

All I could possibly use is beef jerky - and a bottle of Lawry's Seasoned Salt! Any more would break my back.

The "bark" paint sounds good. I'm anxious to see it. What a job. That house is a little big to take on single-handed.

Be sure to congratulate Jodi on her grades. That's real good.

Well, I guess you've got the latest. My finger is healing well. No pain - I'll get it taken care of at Mickey Mouse - the medics are there.

I'll quit for now. Take care all. Thank Niny for the cookies. Darn right I'll eat the crumbs! I doubt if they'll be too smashed. I don't know how long they'll last here though. Nobody gets home-made cookies! What a Niny. Ha!

Heidi sure sounds cute. A real chow-hound! Like her mother.

Tell Sue thanks for the joke - it was a good one!

Bye for now.

Much love, Rome

P.S. Niny, take it easy. And you're not a house painter. If you do paint, go at it like you're saving some of the work for me, ok?

I want you feeling good when I come home.

Mom, still getting out of the house once in awhile? You all need the "rest" - go on a picnic or something, ok?

I worry about you all, so take care, and especially go easy on the house painting, ok?

I'll hold you to it.

Tell Jodi the funnies were much appreciated - they're rare too. Thanks Jodi, keep writing, ok? And do real good on your piano lessons and all so you can play for me in a few months. I'd like to hear you play.

Bye again.

◇◇◇◇◇

- » **Rested at Kontum and Pleiku.**
- » **Promoted and awarded the coveted Combat Medics Badge (CMB).**
- » **Registered his .45.**
- » **In the field at L.Z. Alamo, near L.Z. Brillo Pad and L.Z. Flower Power.**
- » **Showered in "running water" that poured off roof; there's flooding.**
- » **Describes and treats his own terrible cold.**
- » **107 days remaining.**
- » **Encloses a doctor bill.**

Monday
June 24th

Dear family -

I'm fine - just busy. I've been to Kontum and Pleiku for a rest and despite the relaxation, I've had very little time to write. Usually I only go as far as Kontum, but I wanted to register my .45 auto pistol. I found out that I must have more than 60 days left in Nam, but no more than 70 or 75. So I'll have to go back. I had a few beers, saw a U.S.O. show and got a warm shower - about 10 as a matter of fact. I had a great stay, made SP/4 (E-4) and was awarded the Combat Medics Badge (CMB) - rather coveted here.

Collaborator's comment: The coveted Combat Medics Badge was awarded to Jackson for performing medical duties while attached to an infantry unit engaged in active ground combat while he was personally present and under fire. (Code of Federal Regulations §587.70.) He also received a Vietnam Service Ribbon with two bronze stars for serving in two campaigns, including TET. He qualified for The Gallantry Cross, issued by the Republic of South Vietnam, and had to find his own medal in a thrift store, since South Vietnam lost the war. He says that the Good Conduct Medal is "conspicuously absent": the constant threats by Lt. Dufus to send him to the Lon Bin Jail for insubordination might account for this even though his arrest record for failure to board the plane to Vietnam had "mysteriously" gone missing from his file.

I'm back in the field, this time at L.Z. Alamo. I could best tell you where it is by saying it's 1000 meters from L.Z. "Brillo Pad" - where the big fire-fight was that I watched from Hill 830 - L.Z. Flower Power. That was about a month ago, and there hasn't been anything going on since then. It's very quiet.

It's raining and literally flooding outside. My bunker is open on 2 sides, and I'm dry and comfortable, but I did get a shower, wash my hair and brush my teeth - I have running water! It pours off the roof, so I just crouched in the entrance and washed up. I feel great.

I had a terrible cold - it lasted 48 hours. I prescribed penicillin 400,000 units, 4 times a day, 9 am - 1 pm - 5 pm & 9 pm around the clock, along with Erethromycin 9 - 1 - 5 - 9. It sure knocked it. A little trick I learned at Ft. Ord on the pneumonia ward. I forced fluids with the orange & apple juice you sent and backed that up with the vitamins. I feel fine today. I'd have been sick for at least 10 days normally. I'd never had such a terrible cold. I had the Dr. look at my throat before I left Kontum and he said it was definitely infected but it didn't look like tonsillitis. I told him about how they used to act up and the glands swell, ears plug up etc., and he agreed that my ears have small canals - slightly inflamed, but he said I was probably catching a bad cold. He was right. It's all gone now.

Collaborator's comment: The number of respiratory problems Jackson treated in his men, plus the fact that Agent Orange is known to cause respiratory illness, leaves one wondering about all these "colds" the men caught in Vietnam.

Nothing is new. I guess we'll be on Alamo for awhile - rumor has it that D Co's mess hall (cooks & tent, stoves (gas) and etc.) is on the way. On Hill 830 we stayed 22 days. Looks good now too.

I'll try to drop Sue and Roger a line, but tell them hello for me. I hope the worst of the painting is done. I'd like to help. Niny, take care. I'm doing likewise. Jodi, be good, and practice your piano lessons. I'll be home soon (107 days) to see how you're doing.

Take care all, write.

Much love, Rome

P.S. Enclosed is a bill from Dr. Littlehales - I told Nik you'd agreed to pay it but I didn't know. Do send it to her if you aren't going to pay it so we can, ok? Thanks.

◇◇◇◇◇

» **Writing while sitting down on patrol outside perimeter.**
» **Wants Blitz beer. Doc and Gardner miss Blitz.**
» **Wants cookies, salami, beef jerky, BBQ chips, shoulder holster for .45, and Wizard of Id funnies.**

Wed, June 26

Dear family -

We were supposed to leave L.Z. alamo the day before yesterday, but we're still waiting.

Right now I'm on a patrol about 800 yards outside the perimeter. We found a place that looked comfortable and sat down. It beats walking through the bushes.

Not much is new. I've just been sitting around getting shorter. There hasn't been anything else to do. I'll let you know when we move or anything, but for now it's just sit and wait to do something.

I drank the rest of the juice, and I enjoyed it. It's a great help when the water is so bad and it's so hot. If you do send more, only send 1 or 2 cans from now on, because it's heavy and I can't drink it as fast as you send it. I do share it, but I keep a few cans in my pack just in case we don't get water. The only food I need is cookies and some beef jerky or salami - some kind of good meat like that. Your pkgs. get here in 5 to 7 days, so if I need anything, I'll tell you. I don't need sox now because I got some in Kontum at the supply tent, and I still have some that you sent. I just don't want you to over-do the food etc. because it builds up faster than I can eat it or share it.

I'll tell you what would be just great. Once a week, say Monday, send a pkg: 3, 4, 5, 6, ? cans of Blitz beer, a roll of salami or beef jerky and something like barbeque flavored corn chips, or ? Then I could sit down on Sat. nite, have a few beers, some beef jerky and something to snack on. That's all I need. Maybe you could pack it with one pair of sox. Once a week would be perfect! That'd work much better. And if Niny just happens to make some cookies or ? you could send some besides the weekly care pkg. Ok?

I cleaned your camera real good last nite. Lenses with alcohol and I dusted it inside with a Q-tip deal. I used the infra-red, and I'm shooting good 'ol black & white.

If you can find a shoulder holster for a .45 auto. pistol, pick it up ($8 - $10 very plain, black, & cheap) and I'll send you a $ order, ok?

Don't breathe a word of "we sent Rome..." Like you said -

In case you're wondering, Blitz beer is Portland's own, and there are 2 of us here who "miss Blitz." Steve Gardner from S.E. side, a chemistry grad from O.S.U., 24 yrs old & drives a new Corvette. Great guy, one of my best friends.

I want to do some "sketching" while I have time out here, so I'll quit for now.

Take care all. Don't worry about me. Everything is fine. 106 days left. 107?

Tell Sue & Roger & Heidi hello for me. I finally wrote to Sue, but I told them I couldn't guarantee another letter soon. I'll try.

I hope you're still getting away from "the Hill" once in awhile. Don't let the painting tie you down.

Please tell Neiheisers hello for me - give them my best.

Tell Jodi to send me some "B.C." or "Wizard of Id" funnies if she can find them. They're great. I just howled at that stupid king's guard who tried on the enemy uniform then stood in front of the window. Jodi will tell you about it.

Niny, take it easy and save something for me to do around there. I miss you all.

Take care, some more.

Bye for now.

Much love, Rome

Collaborator's comment: Jackson mentioned another Portlander, Steve Gardner, in this letter. He recalls several significant events regarding Gardner.

First, Gardner was well educated and smart, with a college degree in chemistry. Jackson notes the irony that the Army doesn't know how to use its resources. Instead of having Gardner do something worthwhile involving his education, the Army:

> takes the smartest guy in our unit and makes him walk point, so he's the most likely to get killed.

The second story involves sleeping in bunkers made of sandbags. To build a bunker, they would dig a hole and fill bags with the dirt. Then they'd build beams across the top to hold the sandbags on the roof. Then they'd build walls and make the roof several bags deep to cushion the shock of incoming mortars. But the sandbags leave enough space in the nooks and crannies for critters to hide there. One night when they were all asleep in a bunker, Gardner starts screaming bloody murder. He thought he was under attack, but it was a rat that had fallen from the ceiling right onto his chest. Those were some huge rats, too.

Another story shows how they got the beams for the roof from local trees. There was a little guy in their unit who had a round head like Charlie Brown. His name was Dewey, so they called him Admiral Dewey. Admiral Dewey liked to blow things up. He was a real powder monkey. They used trees for beams in the bunkers, and in order to knock the trees down, Admiral Dewey would wrap DET cord (detonation cord) around them at the base of the trunk. So one time he wrapped the DET cord a little too well, and when he set it off, the tree shot high off the ground and was heading straight for Gardner. Jackson saw that Gardner was panicked and couldn't tell which way to run to get out from under the flying tree. He was zigging and zagging and it was clear the tree would come down and kill him, so Jackson ran under the tree himself, grabbed Gardner by the arm and pulled him to safety. The very top of the tree did come down on both of them, but those branches were small, so Gardner only got a scratch. Jackson was not even cut. A small limb landed between them.

Later, Gardner ETS'd before Jackson. ETS means elapsed time of service, and refers to his discharge date. Jackson gave Gardner his mother's address, and Gardner visited her and told her how Jackson saved his life from the flying tree.

Another event shows Gardner's resourcefulness. Jackson says:

> One night at a MASH unit Gardner pretended he was a lieutenant and he went into the officer's club — an improvised tent structure. He said his men had just come in from the boonies and he asked if we could come in. He got the okay and we all drank beer and got drunk. I was helping a drunk stagger back to the unit and somebody shouted, "Halt." We ID'd ourselves, and he said, "Do you know where you are?" We were in front of an M16 machine gun position, outside the perimeter. I don't know how we got there. I thought we were navigating in the right direction, but we must have been too drunk.

◇◇◇◇◇

» **Got the early out to start college in the fall. 60 days left.**
» **Called Nickie from the Military Assistance Radio Station (MARS).**
» **In the rear, doing annoying chores, but "beats living like an animal."**
» **Hopes their new lieutenant is not like the ignorant Dufus.**
» **Gil called Nickie a bitch, and "he'll beg to die" when Jackson gets to him.**

Sunday July 7, p.m.

Dear family,

I guess Nickie told you I called. I came to Pleiku to get the early out, which I very successfully did, so I thought I'd use the Mars station.

Collaborator's comment: Mars is the military assistance radio station, where soldiers talk on a ham radio, and volunteers relay the radio message to the States.

I'll E.T.S. [elapsed time of service] (be discharged from the Army) Sept. 13, home Sept. 6th. How's that?

The "brass" was pleased with the P.C.C. letter [Portland Community College admission letter], and I was congratulated by the C.O. and he walked around his desk and walked over to me to shake my hand. He doesn't get up for much.

I sign the papers tomorrow.

I can't believe it yet. I now have 60 days left in the Army. Did Nickie do this? It's great!

I'm just sitting around here "resting." I've been real lucky about that - gotten lots.

I'll be out of the field for good as soon as the Dr. gets off R & R - 10 to 15 days. Then the "war" will be over, for me.

There's a lot of B.S. to put up with back here. Like details, cheap chores, and guard. But I guess it's worth it. Beats living like an animal.

There isn't much I can tell you about what I'm doing. The co. has been on perimeter guard at Dak-To for a week or so. Originally we were going to a firebase 3 kilometers from Cambodia, but at the last second they changed the plans. So I was just goofing off in Dak-To until the papers from school got here. Rumors say we're going to an L.Z. somewhere to sit for awhile. There will be small patrols going out around the perimeter, but it's halfway permanent. No hiking around like before.

We got a Lt. as a platoon leader. He's ok so far, but I hope he doesn't end up like "Dufus," our last Lt. He was too ignorant to be true.

Nothing is new here, except for the early out. That's enough news to last a year! I just can't believe it. I'll be in a classroom instead of being shot at. It doesn't seem possible. I'll still have to see it to believe it.

Tell Sue & Roger hello for me. Also Neiheisers.

I hope the painting is done by now.

Oh, I wonder if you've heard about our friend Gil. He got into an argument with Nickie and called her a bitch. That's one word you don't use around the Jacksons unless it's directed at the Bitch. I finally got so mad I wrote Gil a letter, and I sincerely promised him I'd beat him half to death. I told him that if I ever see him I'll cut him down - with my bare hands. So help me God he'll beg to die. I'm going to break his collar bones first, then one arm, then I'm going to stomp right on his face. I swear this. I just hope he stays around, he'll pay for every word he said.

I can't believe Gil. He's just too much. He's the filthiest crawling form of scum. He's been here, and he should know what it's like. And he does this! I just can't wait to get my hands on him.

Have you talked to him? Why would he do this?!

I won't say anymore. Gil knows the score. He's going to get a lesson in friendship. Only 60 more days. I've even quit smoking to get in shape for this. His "stalling" started it, mouthing off to Nickie finished it.

Collaborator's comment: This anger at Gil impressed the gunner Tweety Bird so much that he later wrote to Jackson to ask if he ever killed the guy.

I managed to get a shower. It won't be long until I'll be living like this permanently.

I guess I'll quit for now.

Take care all. Don't work hard, and be sure to get out of the house. Niny, you take care, ok?

Jodi, take care of Josephine, and be good.

Much love, Rome

◇◇◇◇◇

» **Domestic bills.**
» **When medics are short, they're sent to the rear, but Jackson sent on three-day patrol with only 51 days left.**
» **Jungle rot on feet.**
» **Jackson looks old.**
» **Son Blane talks now.**
» **Plan to unwind for a day or two when he arrives home.**
» **Wants to study art and to paint.**
» **"Going hunting" from firebase 31.**

Monday, July 15th

Dear family,

I'm glad Nickie and Blane came over for dinner, and picked up the T.V. She tells me Sears wants $65 in back pmnts. But it's taken care of at least. Tell Niny I'll pay that bill for Dr. Little-hales. She can't pay a $45 Dr. bill when she only gets $37 or so. So I'll pay her back.

If you'll send me a roll of 35 mm. color film (slides or prints - whichever you like) I'll take picts. of me (a buddy will take them) and send them to you. I'm out of color film. One roll B&W left. I look older, and I am worn and tired and filthy.

153

About everyone here is I guess. That never killed anyone, so I'm fine. I'm scared to death now, because all medics are permanently removed from the field and are given jobs in the rear (aid stations, hospitals etc.) when they reach 90 days left in Nam. I have 51 and I have to go on a 3 day patrol thru enemy infested jungle. It'll be a miracle if I make it back. That's why I look old! If the Army hasn't contacted Nickie by the time you get this, you'll know I made it. I'm going to jump on somebody until they get me out of the toolies. I'm supposed to be relaxing in the rear, in clean clothes, curing my jungle rot and enjoying being short and getting ready to come home. I've fought this damned war every inch of the way. Come hell or high water I'll make it.

> Collaborator's comment: Jackson still has pockmarks on the soles of his feet from jungle rot. He says:

> We never took our boots off because you don't want to get caught without your boots on. But we got jungle rot that way. I have it to this day. It's like the bumpy surface of a sponge on the bottoms of my feet — like craters within craters. It's not causing me problems now. I first went to the VA about it when I got my cluster of Parkinson's symptoms. It sometimes flared up into huge white patches. The whole heel gets huge craters. At first they told me it was just from dirty feet, like a hippie. That made me so mad. I knew what it was, and they didn't.

Yes, I got the early out. At least the Company Cmndr. assures me I will. I won't believe it until I see DROS orders. (Date Returned from Overseas.) My new ETS [Elapsed Time of Service, meaning end service date] is Sept 6th. I'm going to spend a day, maybe 2 relaxing at home before I do any visiting etc. I have a lot of unwinding to do.

> Collaborator's comment: When I read this last paragraph to Jackson, I laughed and said, "Did a couple of days do it for you, or are you still working on that 'unwinding'?" Jackson, who readily acknowledges his PTSD, laughed along with me on realizing he had underestimated the time it would take him to unwind by at least forty-six years.

I didn't know that Blane talks. [Blane is Jackson's toddler son.] I guess there are lots of things I don't know.

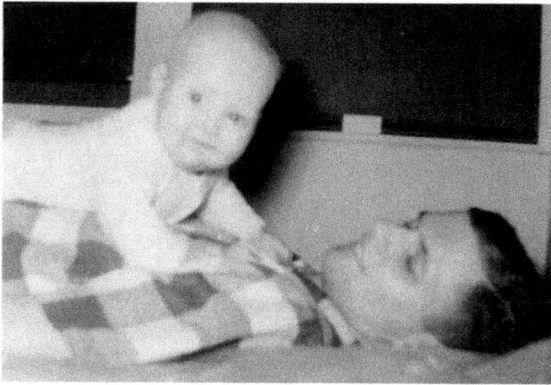

I tried to get "A Light from a Source..." at Ft. Lewis, but I left too soon. It only came off the press in January.

I hope you're feeling well by now. I also hope that painting is done. Speaking of painting, I wish I could do one. I'm running over with ideas. I plan to take some art at PCC - if I ever get there.

Collaborator's comment: It was many years before Jackson

took an oil painting class at Portland State University, but once he began, he produced a prolific amount of work in a short time — large canvases with tranquil, remote scenes, some with birds, but no human figures except a surreal, shadowy face of Chief Joseph in one, inspired by the Chief's famous opposition to the U.S. Cavalry.

I don't need anything. I'd like a few cans of apple & orange juice & a can of Dennison's Chili (hot). I need more Sea & Ski badly. I have enough clean sox, considering I'll be going in soon.

From Pleiku (when I called) I returned to Dak-To, then the co. moved to the toolies the next day. I'm on firebase 31, overlooking a valley which contains a good R & R center & hospital - somewhere. That's why we're going hunting.

Collaborator's comment: "Going hunting" refers to a search and destroy mission to seek out the enemy, kill him, and add him to the U.S.'s body count.

This hill looks so much like Council Crest [a wooded hill in the center of Portland, Oregon] it's scary. It overlooks Dak-Sen which looks like the Raleigh Hills area from Council Crest, and even the hills are the same, except no Portland. We have generators (gas) up here = elec. lites, ice, etc. Not bad. I live in a bunker as usual when on a firebase; it's comfortable as bunkers go. We don't have electric lites in the bunker. Just the big-wigs who live here. Typical.

I'm fine. Take care, write.

Love you all, Rome

P.S. Tell Niny & Jodi a special hello. Tell Niny to take care, Jodi be good. Be home soon. Got your pkg. day b'fore yesterday. Loved it too. Keep it up. Tell Sue & Roger hello, also Joanne & family.

» **Has new Polaroid camera.**
» **Jackson and Tweety Bird crash Army chaplains' fried chicken dinner.**
» **In Dak-To they were hit with rockets and mortar fire.**
» **Will head to Ban Me Thout.**
» **Will return and be released September 17.**

Collaborator's comment: On the outside of this envelope Jackson wrote "51 days," the time he had left to serve. Also, on all his envelopes, he handwrote the word "free" where postage would normally go — free postage being one small benefit of being in the Army. On another envelope that he had sealed with a strip of medical bandage he wrote, "Humidity - these envelopes seal themselves!"

Tuesday, July 30

Dear family -

After I called you this morning I got cleaned up and fooled around all day. I got paid, so I went to the p.x., and for some reason they were well stocked - so I got a Polaroid Swinger - a $19.95 camera, for $9.95 and I got 9 rolls of film for it, so you'll be getting lots of picts. From now on, send a roll of "Swinger" #20 film - the Argus is locked up in the 1/35 Medics' Supply trailer.

After dinner I showed some guys how to get the MARS station, and then a friend from Niagara Falls [Tweety Bird] and I stopped into the new Service Club to write a letter. By luck, again, tonite is the 193rd anniversary of Army Chaplains, and we walked right into it. Col. Sanders' Kentucky Fried Chicken, cold Pepsi, baked beans, potato salad, apple pies, - the works. So I'm sitting here, too full to get up, drinking a cold Pepsi. This buddy and I laughed so hard we almost croaked at how we've lived. These are adventures only we could appreciate, especially when we're living in Pleiku for these few days, warm, dry and well fed.

Incidentally, I'm in Pleiku (they wouldn't allow any mention of places, moves, etc. on the phone). We were in Dak-To long enough to get hit by 122mm rockets and 81mm mortar fire, then we moved to Kontum. We were there for 2 days, then we got on a convoy to Pleiku. We're on a 5 day "stand-down" which could end at any time, before moving to Ban Me Thout - way south of here. There is very little going on down there, and it's sure to be better; the land is flat for one thing, and the monsoon is nearly over.

Collaborator's comment: Jackson tells a story about a time when they were under mortar fire in their bunkers:

During the mortar attacks Eddie B. became a war hero. He had lots of other medals, but he wanted a Purple Heart, so he would stick his head up to try to catch shrapnel, and he did. Admiral Dewey called, "Medic!" and told me that Eddie had metal in his eye. There was an 81 mm mortar shard in the sack under his eyes. It looked like a dime with ragged edges. I worked on it and got it out and wrote "81 mm mortar, purple heart" and gave him a red tag ticket out of there. We'd pop yellow smoke to show the helicopters where to land for medivacs.

I received orders on my early out. My E.T.S. [elapsed time of service] is now Sept. 24th. I have to return from Nam 7 days prior - therefore, September 17th. Once I arrive at Fort Lewis, on Sept 17th, I will be automatically released - or discharged, regardless of E.T.S. So I will be a civilian upon return from overseas (D.R.O.S.) [date returned from overseas] or Sept 17th. Ok? Ok.

Needless to say, everything is fine. I miss you all very much, and I worry about you being sick. I don't want you worrying about me, cuz I'm fine.

I'm fine, except for this floor is getting hard, so I'll quit for now. Take care, please, and don't worry.

Much love all, Rome

◇◇◇◇◇

» **South on convoy to Ban Me Thout, then into the hills.**
» **Rain and leeches and filth.**
» **Needs rain jacket sent to replace rotted one.**
» **Needs canned heat for cooking.**
» **Wants dry socks, foot powder, sweatshirts, old towel for cleaning weapon, instant coffee, Pream, hard candy, cigars, canned bacon, two whetstones, Nestle's Quick, cream of tomato soup, Benson & Hedges menthol cigarettes.**

Collaborator's comment: The envelope of the following letter is filthy with smeared mud, front and back, and the letter inside is grimy.

Monday, Aug. 5th

Dear family -

After I called from Pleiku [by use of MARS relayed radio] I got on a convoy headed south to Ban Me Thout. We spent one nite there, then moved to a hill and set up camp. We spent one nite there, then we headed for the toolies. That's where I am now - a million miles up in the hills. The rain and leeches make it almost unbearable- especially since my rain jacket literally rotted from this humidity, and fell apart. Please send another one. This

163

time, size: Large to X-Large, and long; like to the knees if possible, and the material must be like canvas. I'll cover the cost. Right now I'd give $75 for one like I need. Long and tough. They make rain jackets almost like canvas, and long too. Help? Please send it quick.

That chili sure would go good. I haven't gotten a letter since July 30; or a pkg. either.

I'm fine, just filthy, leech bitten and wet. We'll be going to a fire base in a few days, so I'll be able to get dry etc.

What on earth were you talking about: "an explosion near sandbags in my own area?" or something. We're always blasting trees, logs, rocks, blowing bunkers or something. It's nothing to worry about.

> Collaborator's comment: Here's an example of how they were always blowing things up, especially trees which were used for beams for sandbag bunkers. Jackson recalls:

> We had dug a fresh pit for a pit toilet and we carved out the lid of an ammo box with a hatchet for the seat. Meanwhile Admiral Dewey wanted to cut a tree to use for beams for the bunkers. So he wrapped it at the base a couple of times with DET cord (detonation cord). Several wraps around the tree would have done it. Dewey put on a couple of extra wraps for good luck — and maybe one or two more to make sure he got the job done. And he set it off. And the air was instantly filled with wood slivers of all sizes — the tree was blown apart. The tree went straight up — severed at the ground — and the butt end

of it came down on the crapper that we'd just finished. We had to start over with a new latrine.

Admiral Dewey looked like Charlie Brown in Peanuts — curly hair, slightly balding in the middle, short, medium weight. He was very unlike an Admiral. He got the nickname because his name was Dewey. He liked to blow things up — a real powder monkey.

Please send something to cook with. "Canned heat" or ? - anything! I'd sell my soul for a cup of hot coffee or choc., and I have C's (rats.) to make both. A large jar of instant coffee & Pream too. Some hard candy, and some cigars. They make canned bacon too - send "heat" and I'll cook it on a coffee can lid!

Just anything you run across that'd be good in the toolies. Picture yourself camping in the jungle during the monsoons and go from there, ok? I sure could use more dry socks too. Those were a life saver. Also foot powder. And 2 of my sweatshirts with P.S.C. on them or whatever it is. Don't buy any, just send those, ok? An old towel or sheet for cleaning weapons. Mud and water is hell out here, and I'd like to have a clean weapon. Send 2 whetstones, you know, the small ones, 1" x 3" or so. Not that roller deal. A small can of Nestle's Quick. Cream of Tomato Soup, a carton of Benson & Hedges menthol cigs.

Maybe you could find some kind of burner at the Wigwam - remembering that I can't get gasoline. They should have something, there'd be heat, cooking, and lite.

It shouldn't take long to get the rain jacket here - that's all I really need.

I gotta go eat, so I'll quit for now.

Take care; love you all.

Much love, Rome

Collaborator's comment: While in "the toolies" they would sometimes run into unpleasant animal life, beyond the ever present leeches and mosquitoes, and the piss ants that swarmed him on his first morning in country. Jackson recalls a couple of startling animal encounters:

> Once, while we were eating, somebody yelled. A poisonous bamboo viper came too near. A guy with a .45 tried to shoot it but missed. Then a cook with an entrenching tool chopped its head off. They dried it, and I still have a piece of it about the size of a dollar bill. It's framed in my display case with my medals. (An entrenching tool is a folding shovel.)

> Another time we had a close encounter with a huge tarantula. We were walking in single file down a steep, muddy, wet hill. The guy who was two men in front of me slipped and fell, and almost sat on it. The guy in front of me squashed it with a rifle butt. I had to walk around it. It was as big as Eli's head." (Eli is Jackson's part terrier rescue dog.)

◇◇◇◇◇

» **Near Pleiku at The Oasis, a base camp.**
» **Dull but NOT the boonies.**
» **Trying to get out of the field, because he's short.**
» **Has bad cold.**
» **Tells mother who Steve Gardner is.**
» **Describes weapons Steve carries while walking point.**
» **The absurdity of Steve, who is an honor grad in chemistry, Preacher, a licensed minister, and Teach, a school teacher, being assigned as point and flank men.**
» **Three dead, five wounded when Colonel couldn't get help to a platoon on recon.**
» **Needs rain jacket and film.**

Sunday, Aug 11th

Dear family -

This'll be short, but it's an effort anyway. I'm in a place near Pleiku called The Oasis. It's just a base camp of some kind.

Our company went north, and this platoon came here. I guess we'll be here 10 days or so, going on small patrols and stuff like that. It's just like being in Pleiku, except there's nothing here like a club or MARS station or etc. It's dull, raining, muddy, and generally depressing, but it's not the boonies, so I don't mind. In 29 days I'll go to Pleiku to start processing to come home, so I feel short. I still might find a way to get out of the field a few days before that, but it doesn't look good.

I have another bad cold, but it's just from being wet all the time and sleeping in the mud. I'm taking forty thousand pills a day. The Dr. just came in on a convoy; the medics are in the process of moving from Ban Me Thout back to Kontum. I'll see him in the a.m. and yell about being short. For all the good it'll do. Everyone is outraged at the idea of me being in the field with 35 (or so) days left in the Army! 12 more men go home before Aug. 26th, all medics, all had jobs in the rear. This had better make an opening for me or I'll see the Colonel.

You asked about Steve Gardner. He lives in S.E. Portland, Westmoreland, and he dated Kathee for several years. [Jackson describes Kathee as "a slutty high school pal." Jackson had a relationship with her before, and later, only briefly, after the war. Gardner told Jackson that Kathee "did everyone on the Oklahoma State wrestling team."] He [Gardner] walks point - or lead man for our platoon. If there's a mine or booby trap or a stake pit or ?, Steve will "find" it, one way or another.

> Collaborator's comment: stake pits are one of the booby traps built by enemy forces by digging a hole in the ground, sharpening bamboo sticks, and staking them in the hole which is hidden by shrubbery, so a person who steps there falls in and gets skewered on the stakes.

He carries around 400 rounds of M-16 ammo, and he's the only man authorized to carry his weapon on fully auto at all times.

He carries C.S. (riot) gas grenades and fragmentation grenades, and assorted other weapons designed to counter an ambush or surprise attack. Steve is followed by an M-79 grenade launcher, also carried off "safe." It fires frag. grenades, gas, bee-hive rounds (1000 pin-head size fragments that have a positive kill radius of 50 meters), and fire-cracker rounds (10 small bombs that scatter before exploding), all packed in the grenade that the M-79 fires. The M-79 adapts to fire 12 gauge shotgun .00 buckshot too. So now you know what Steve does. Steve is an honor grad of O.S.U., chemistry. See? I told Jim his education won't help. They'll high pressure him and promise him all sorts of crap, and he'll end up like Steve. Would you walk "point" in Nam? A point man's life expectancy is 1 1/2 seconds. Mine is 8 seconds. (In a fire fight.) I told Jim he shouldn't get out of the service, but he'd better use his head. I'd give anything if he could see what I see in just 24 hours.

The Colonel's calculations were off a little today. He sent a platoon on recon, and could not get them help in time. 3 dead, 5 seriously wounded this afternoon. I wonder how many had degrees, or were honor grads. We have a licensed minister and a 25 year old school teacher with 3 yrs. of teaching behind him. "Preacher" walks point when Steve doesn't. Joe Driscole, "Teach" is a flank man and carries an M-79 grenade launcher. James had better use his head before he gets it blown off.

I've been real lucky. I'm in the right place when everyone else gets in trouble. The right company, and the "best" platoon. Like being here at the Oasis. The rest of the co. is near Kontum. On the way, on the convoy, they received 3 rounds of sniper fire. I was in a dry tent napping. I suppose I'll be here another week, then this platoon will be going to Kontum to join the company.

I don't expect any trouble at all, and I hope I get out of the field.

I'm sitting around in a supply tent because they have electric lites. I guess I'll write a letter to Nickie, so I'll quit for now.

Tell Niny to take care, and Jodi. Tell Sue, Roger, and Heidi Grit hi for me.

Much love, Rome

P.S. That wasn't me in the paper.

I patched up my rain jacket with some tape I found, so it should last another 10 or 15 days. Hurry with the rain "dress." Those camouflaged duck hunting deals are good, green or brown. They're long, anyway, and tough enough to last here.

Bye for now. I'll write soon.

Send some "Swinger" #20 film & I can send picts. I bought one in Pleiku.

◇◇◇◇◇

» **On light duty at The Oasis, medically restricted with bronchitis.**
» **28 days left in 'Nam, 35 in the Army.**

Tues., Aug 13th

Mom, Niny & Jodi,

I have to go pick up a truck in about 20 minutes so this won't be much of a letter. I'm at the Oasis just outside Pleiku, and I'm just taking it easy. I guess I told you they found out I've got bronchitis, so I'm not going on any patrols or anything. I'm medically "restricted" to light duty in the camp area. I've been driving a 3/4 ton truck around checking guards along the perimeter - I don't even get out of the truck.

I didn't have any luck getting out of the field - but I guess it doesn't matter.

I mailed your camera to Nickie this a.m. - I left it with the medics to take care of. They took care of it alright. The shutter was broken and the spring that cocks it is messed up. I could've shot somebody! I'll have it repaired, cleaned and checked on before I return it so it's in perfect shape. It couldn't be helped - on my part.

I'm doing fine, so don't worry. I'm eating like a horse here - lots of hot chow. I've quit coughing, and I just have a cold now - it's going away.

Take care of yourselves and don't worry about me. In 28 days I'll be leaving Nam. 35 days left in the Army.

Must run.

Tell the Grists hello, Joanne & family too.

Bye for now,

Much love, Rome

P.S. It's pouring rain and blowing just like it does at Timberline just before the snow. Cold? Wow! It's about 70° here! Ha! I'm freezing. Guess I'm used to 115° heat while carrying a pack.

Be home soon.

Collaborator's comment: Jackson's "light duty" at The Oasis was also assigned so he wouldn't have to accompany the others into danger when he was short. He says:

> We were sent to Ban Mc Thout, but I didn't want to be in danger because I was getting short. So I was told I could stay at the "Oasis" which was an ammo dump on the way there. I could have stayed in comfortable barracks with the other guys, but I didn't want to be around people, so I slept by myself in a cave the whole time I was at the Oasis.

◇◇◇◇◇

» **Photo with a scout dog, trained to kill.**

Thursday, Aug 15th

Dear family -

Sorry these pictures are so lousy, but it's something anyway. This dog, "Rex," is trained to kill. We use him as a scout. He's a good one too. He about pulled my arm off in this one pict.

We're on alert to move at any time, so this'll be short.

Today I have 31 days left. It's hard to believe!

I'm fine. Over my cold etc.

Write, ok?

Take care, love you all.

I'll write as soon as I can.

Bye for now.

Much love, Rome

» **Writing to his married sister, her husband, and their child.**
» **Describes bad last two weeks; sniper fire while on a convoy, plus they got cut off from their perimeter by a platoon of gooks and had to hide.**
» **Got drunk with a tank driver and "road tested" an 11 ton armored personnel carrier. Got tangled in barbed wire and tripped on a tent stake.**
» **Will soon "go in" and wear clean clothes and sleep on a cot.**

Wed, Aug 21st

Roger, Sue, & Heidi,

I'm just south of Pleiku if that tells you anything. The company I'm in had been down in the rice paddy land sloshing in the swamps for about 10 days, then we went to Pleiku. The co. went north and my platoon, 26 guys went south, and we've been here about 10 days. Yesterday the platoon joined the rest of the co. up north and left me here to watch the tent and a bunch of junk we borrowed. I guess I'll meet the co. in a couple of days, but I'm in no hurry. It's nice here - nobody's shooting at me. Today I have 27 days left with Uncle Sugar, so I have no use for playing war.

The last 2 weeks has been real bad. A sniper tried to do us in while we were on a convoy, and every time we move we run into a platoon or co. of gooks. Monday nite a platoon of gooks got between us and our perimeter and we had some fun trying to get back. We hid in a big clump of bushes and set out mines all around us. I guess they gave up on us. Last nite I got drunk with a tank driver from Tacoma, and he and I decided to "road test" this 11 ton armored personnel carrier. Then I drove it for awhile and scared us both so bad we went back to his tent and finished up a case of beer. Then at midnite I started back. It was pouring down rain, like you've never seen it rain until you've seen the monsoons. To help things, I got tangled up in a barbed wire fence, the kind that's rolled like one of those slinky toys. I almost drowned getting out of that, then when I got to the tent I tripped over a tent stake and tore up my shin. I finally crashed on my cot and woke up at noon today. Soaking wet. War is hell. I'd never last if I had more than 27 days left.

On Monday the 26th I'm "going in" for good. They're taking me out of the field and giving me a job in the aid station. So I guess the war is pretty well over for me. It's going to be weird to wear clean clothes and be dry, and bathe more than once a month and sleep on a cot instead of in the mud. I need to practice being civilized and being house-broken.

Collaborator's comment: Jackson never managed to become very domesticated or "housebroken." He has always preferred living in remote locations, and has tended not to invest much in the way of housing. He has lived in his mother's basement, on friends' couches, in a girlfriend's apartment, in a self-constructed cabin in the woods, in a homemade greenhouse, and in a small travel trailer in the woods. He finally lives in a home with indoor plumbing and electricity, but it is far from the sights and sounds of neighbors, ringed by majestic cedar trees, with a natural waterfall on the property. He has never aspired to live in a standard American dream home. He likes campfires and star gazing at night. He does bathe and wear clean clothing now.

I'll arrive in the world Sept. 17th, and I'm supposed to call Nickie when I get to McChord Air Force Base, but I'm going to wait until I get all processed and get my discharge, then I'm going to walk into where she works. She'll faint. I think I'll drop in on Mom and Niny too.

I guess I'd better gather up my junk just in case someone comes after this tent and stuff. I've gotta be ready to get on a chopper and go to wherever the co. is.

Take care and write if you get time.

Tell Mom & Niny I'm fine, and I'll write soon.

See you soon, Rome

P.S. Would you believe I can't find your address? [This letter to Rome's sister and her family was sent care of his mother.]

◇◇◇◇◇

- » **Finally got out of the field; is in Pleiku.**
- » **Plans for R & R in Malaysia.**
- » **Clean clothes, clean writing paper, deodorant, after shave.**
- » **Took medical aid to locals, called MEDCAP.**

Monday, Aug 26th   Got 2 pkgs. Thanx!

Greets -

War's over. Yup, I did it. I'm in Pleiku - to stay! I had to get transferred to an armored unit to do it - (not my doing - 1/35 people felt sorry for me but couldn't otherwise help) - but I have a warm dry bed, sheets, p.x. 1/4 mile away, civilian clothes, hot good food, beer & pop, cleanliness, aftershave lotion, even deodorant! Isn't life great.

I even got an R & R - from Sept 9th to 14th - would you believe Malaysia! Wow. You guessed it. I need $20 or $30 postal money order, ok? My credit's good.

I'm on cloud 9. This is just like stateside duty. I even wear a "white" t-shirt and my jump boots.

Collaborator's comment: Jump boots are more formal leather boots, not good for jungle wear, as opposed to canvas topped jungle boots with holes for water to slosh in and out

179

while walking in swampy conditions. When this collaborator once travelled to a Central American jungle, Jackson advised her to equip herself with jungle boots, and they worked best in those conditions.

Sometimes I drive a jeep - I told 'em I had lots of practice. Ha!

I also drive an 11 ton armored personnel carrier - APC henceforth. It's a ball. Today I went out to take candy to the kids, and medical aid to the people of the villages around Pleiku.

I borrowed (was "forced" to use) a 35 mm camera. Beaucoup slides comin' up!

Somebody up there likes me. The fitin's over.

I'll write tomorrow. All I have is time, and clean dry paper.

Take care. Need I say I'm fine.

Bye for now.

Much love, Beother

Note new address - copy exactly, ok?

I don't need anything. I gots a p.x.

◇◇◇◇◇

- » **Had to go on patrol.**
- » **Runs into high school friend Bill Swanson.**
- » **Goes on MEDCAP again.**
- » **Details of travel home plans.**

Friday, Aug 30th

Mom, Niny, & Jodi,

I had to go on an overnite patrol last nite, but at least when I got back I could take a shower and get some sleep and put on clean clothes - dry.

Believe it or not, when the patrol was forming up to go, Bill Swanson walked up. He's a real tall guy with glasses who was in about half of my high school classes, and in the Errants too. We B.S.ed all nite, and I'm meeting him at the mail club tonite for a celebration. He's a tanker in "A" 1/10 cav.

This pict. is me sitting behind a .50 caliber machine gun on an A.P.C. [armored personnel carrier]. It was taken after our "Med-Cap" the other day (taking medicine etc. to villagers).

Collaborator's comment: MEDCAP stands for Medical Civilian Assistance Program, designed to "win hearts and minds" of the locals.

181

I haven't been doing much. About the hardest thing is taking picts. I have a "Swinger," a 104 and a 35 mm Fujica, which your "slides" are in. I've only shot 8 or 10 exposures - there are a million on a roll. I'll send the first roll soon.

I gave up the R & R in Da Nang - costs too much, and too close to coming home.

If I ever get my pay I'll be ok. They sent it to the 1/35 instead of 1/10 Cav., and my money is out in the boonies. Damned idiots. The p.x. will be sold out of everything by the time I get paid - they ruined my last chance to get a tape deck.

If you want anything, send the money pretty quick. If I can't get it in the p.x., I'll go in Pleiku and buy it from the local economy. Anything from jewels to electronics. Last call.

I got to go on Med-Cap, so bye for now.

Take care. See you soon.

I have my Port-Call!!!!(A port call is where you pick up an overseas flight.)

Flight W2C4 leaves Cam Rahn Bay at 8 p.m. on the 22nd, arrives at McChord A.F.B. at 7 p.m. the 22nd, 16 hours later! I'll be on it.

By your time, I leave Viet Nam at 5 a.m. the 21st, a Saturday. By breakfast time I'll be over Japan. By dinner I'll be over Alaska. Before you finish dinner, I'll be "home." I'll call when I get there, but I won't be out of the Army until the 23rd.

Gotta go.

Much love, Rome

$\diamond\diamond\diamond\diamond\diamond$

» **Doesn't need anything sent.**
» **Plan to surprise Nickie when he gets home.**

Sunday, Sept 1st

Greets -

I'm just sitting around in my clean clothes being short. 20 3/4 days left. I wrote a letter to Charlie, but there's nothing to write.

I got another package today - wow. I don't need anything now. I've got 12 pairs of socks and 2 raincoats, and I "have" to quit smoking before I leave here, so I'll barely smoke all these cigarettes, and I now have two new raincoats.

I've been doodling - just sketches, and I'm a little "rusty." Practice will cure that - time is all I have.

I feel sorry for Kathee. She's "lost" - I'd be with her if I could - and I hate to see her alone, like going to Eugene. Tell her hello for me, tell her to take care.

Collaborator's comment: Later, between wives, Jerome and Kathee did have a brief try at getting together, but he soon rejected her for being a "slob" with dirty children who had hair lice and having a drug dealing brother who put them at risk.

Don't write after, or on the 13th. I'm too SHORT! Ha! Seriously, I wouldn't get a letter mailed after the 12th.

Also, don't send any pkgs., I'm loaded with everything.

I'll be out of the Army on Monday the 23rd, but I don't know what time. It just depends on how long it takes to process. I'll drop by school when I get to Portland.

I guess I told you I'm not going to call Nickie - I'm just going to pick up my discharge, hitch-hike to Portland, and walk into where she works. She "knows" I'll call sometime the 23rd. Should be quite a surprise. I'll drop by once I pick up the car. Don't say anything to her - or Niny, or Jodi either.

Gotta go for now. I'll write tomorrow.

Much love, Rome

P.S. If you haven't gotten a money order yet, don't. I'm not going to Malaysia.

Collaborator's comment: The surprise romantic reunion planned with Nickie never happened. Instead Rome decided to call Nickie and ask her to come and pick him up at Fort Lewis. He waited for her arrival for hours, and she never showed up. Later, she told him she couldn't come because "the baby was asleep." To this day, he cannot bear to watch news reports of servicemen returning home to the arms of enthusiastic wives and children. Only forty-one days after returning home, following an argument "over something stupid," Jackson walked out the door and never returned. Nickie contrived to have him terminate his parental rights to Blane during their divorce, and she kept him from visiting his son for eleven years. She remarried a "lifer" who adopted Blane. When Blane became of age, he came back into his father's life, and Blane's wife now employs Jerome's daughter-in-law Mary in a real estate appraisal business.

Jackson acknowledges that PTSD has prevented him from bonding emotionally with any of the women in his life after the war. When asked if there might have been one he was truly in love with, he said, without hesitation, "Nickie." But he also stayed loyal to Virginia through her ovarian cancer and her dementia, and has worn her wedding ring on his pinkie finger ever since her death.

◇◇◇◇◇

» **Decided not to spend money on R & R.**
» **Refuses to work because he is short.**
» **Enthusiastically describes stereo tape recorder he bought for himself.**
» **Plans for return home include selling one of two new raincoats so he won't be broke on arrival.**

Tuesday, Sept 10th

Mom, Niny and Jodi,

I can't remember what I've told you, but I decided not to take R & R. Why spend all that money to go to Malaysia when I'd be home 7 days later? I would've left yesterday. If the people who sit on their ass in base camp would've gotten in gear and given me an R & R 3 months ago it would've been different. Then I had to move to the 1/10 cav. to even be offered an R & R. That's just the Army. These lifers deserve to re-enlist.

I spent every day in the boonies until I had 19 days left in the Army and still don't get a damned thing to show for it. I told the 1st Sergeant he'd have to put me back in jail before I'd make a formation or go on guard or on a patrol or do anything. I've been in the Army too long and I'm too short to work. I sit and listen to my tape.

Oh yes, I bought a National Panasonic Total Stereo Automatic Reverse 4 track Tape Recorder the other day. I paid for it - $174.00, but it's $280 in the U.S.A. It does everything but walk - automatically. Dual 30 watt speakers, recording level indicators, automatic reverse, it plays one side of a tape on tracks 1 & 3 and automatically reverses at the end of the tape and plays the other side on tracks 2 & 4, automatically switching from channel 1 to channel 2 without missing a note of stereo! It will record from radio, T.V., phono, or even an amplifier; either totally "absorbing" what sounds it records, or it can "monitor" through its own stereo amplifier and still record the "extra" sound coming from its own speakers. It has external jacks for 4 speakers as big as you can find, besides a headphone jack, 2 "mike" jacks for stereo recordings either through a jack or the mikes that came with it. It counts recording time so you can find any song in 3600 feet of recording tape by just finding the numbers (if you keep track of where it is on the tape.) I could go on for 30 pages. You'll have to see it to believe it. It's got a black cabinet with silver trim and a "smoked" glass window that covers the reels etc. It's fantastic!

I had to borrow $40 plus the $50 you sent! Think Nickie will kill me? I do. I went thru too much out there not to get something to relax by, and this "R & R" will last for a lifetime.

> Collaborator's comment: Jackson loves music, and he missed it over there. He remembers hearing live music once and even recalls the song they were playing:

> At some unknown MASH unit I heard two guitars being played in a tent. I stuck my head in. They said it was called "Little Black Egg." It was the first good live music I had heard in ages. I had never heard it before, and not again until just now when we listened to it on YouTube.

With all the marital problems over debts and loan payments, Jackson didn't learn until he arrived home that Nickie had also made several large purchases without prior discussion. With scorn in his voice after all these years, Jackson reported to this collaborator that Nickie had bought a new couch with a "space age" design to its arms, and she had arranged to buy herself "new boobs." None of this boded well for the marriage that lasted only 41 days after Doc's return to the U.S.

The tape recorder that was supposed to provide a lifetime of musical pleasure was stolen a year later in a home burglary.

I guess I told you my plane lands at McChord Air Force Base at 6 p.m. the 22nd. It's going to take 36 to 48 hours to process out of the Army. Nickie will be on her vacation, so we're going to the beach as soon as I can get out, & stop by P.C.C. [Portland Community College] and register. I'll stop by the house (or school) for awhile, then I'm going to go unwind for a few days.

This Sunday I start clearing this place, and the Sunday after that I'll be home.

I got a cholera and a plague shot yesterday. I'm running a temp of 100.4 so I'm not doing much. I'll be over it tomorrow.

I sold my Polaroid for $8 to buy stuff I have to have for my uniform. I have 20¢ to get home on. I should be able to draw a few dollars before I clear finance.

You asked if I got the pkgs. you sent. I got one with socks and another raincoat. I hope you didn't send anything after that. I don't need anything, and I'm almost packed. I'm going to sell one raincoat so I won't be completely broke. I guess I'll go sit in the sun for awhile. I'm pale after all these typhoons. That didn't last long. It's rained for weeks and 2 typhoons have hit. I haven't seen the sun since July. I guess I won't either, until I get home.

Tell everyone hello for me. I'd do as you suggested, Mom, but I'm broke. I'll see what I can do.

Take care everyone. I will too, and I'll see you the 23rd or 24th. I'll call from Ft. Lewis the 22nd.

Bye for now,

Much love, Beother

Thanx for the funnies Jodi. See you real soon!

◇◇◇◇◇

» **Last letter home.**
» **Rocket rounds just as he's preparing to leave 'Nam.**

Fri. Sept. 13th

Greets,

Tomorrow morning I start clearing Pleiku. Sunday I leave Vietnam. I guess that's the latest.

9 rocket rounds came in Wed. or Thurs. nite but they all fell short. All it did was cause a lot of commotion.

> Collaborator's comment: He didn't tell the truth to his family. Four men in perimeter bunkers were killed, and several rounds went over his head and hit the mess hall. He wasn't called in as medic because they were killed and went to "graves registration," a refrigerated unit where the dead were kept.

I guess I'll go into Pleiku tomorrow after I've processed everywhere I can, and do some "shopping."

I guess I've told you about everything I can. There isn't too much to tell about sitting around.

I'll be home in a day or 2 after you get this letter.

Take care.

Love much, Rome

Collaborator's comment: After returning home, Jerome Jackson corresponded with Tweety Bird, a machine gunner who remained in Vietnam. Following are the three letters Tweety Bird sent him, with spelling and punctuation as written. Jerome explains:

> We called him Tweety Bird because his boots were two sizes too big, and he had a shock of curly blond hair, so he looked and walked just like Tweety Bird.

$$\diamondsuit\diamondsuit\diamondsuit\diamondsuit\diamondsuit$$

» **The medic who replaced Jackson is wounded in a firefight.**

Nov. 5, 68

Hi Doc,

Well, how the hell are you. I'm still making it. I don't know how, but Im still alive. I hope this letter fines you an your beautiful family the same. I finally recieved your most welcome letter. What took you so long "wow" I thought you forgot about Nam. But know one can forget this joint.

You said in your letter that the world has changed. Boy I hope its for the better. It sure can't get any worse. Well now instead of SP/4 Jackson it's Mr. Jackson boy it must be great.

An here I thought you were a lifer. Ha Ha.

Collaborator's comment: Because Jackson was older and had served longer than other soldiers, they called him Grandpa, and might have confused him with a lifer. He says:

They called me Grandpa because I was twenty-two and had been in the Army three years. I enlisted when I was nineteen. Most of the guys were younger because, as draftees, they only had two years to serve.

You know I'm a nosey person. But what ever happened to that guy you were going to kill when you got home? Boy I never saw you so dam mad. I'm glad to here your doing so well.

> Collaborator's comment: Tweety Bird refers to Gil, the fellow who was supposed to help Jackson get enrolled in college, but who stole the tuition deposit, called Nickie a bitch, and disappeared.

Well guess what Doc. We had our first fire fight.

An we only lost two men an one seriously wounded. He was the medic that took your place. We recovered over fifty ruck sacks about 200 rockets an grenades. Plus I don't know how many dinks. Well, Iv got to run now. We finally got some clean clothes. So I think I'll try an get some.

By for now.

Say hello to your beautiful wife an child for me.

Your machine gunner,

Tweety Bird.

◇◇◇◇◇

- » **Lanky back from R & R.**
- » **Preacher and Jim Humphrey killed on patrol.**
- » **Tweety Bird out of the field with bad feet.**
- » **Revenewer in the hospital with malaria.**
- » **Polite in Japan.**
- » **Cliff remains with "bad eyes."**

Nov. 20, 68

From LZ Jean
Hi Doc,

Well how the hell are you. I hope fine.

Hows school coming along. You aint back in the Army yet. "Ha Ha"

Lankies still here he just got back from R & R an he told me to tell you that he said hi. I finally got out of the field for good. Remember my dam feet where giving me so much trouble, well they finally broke down for good now. I don't no if you here much about this place but where really hitting the shit. Do you remember Preacher & Jim Humphry well they both were killed last week. Boy I still can't believe it.

Last night we took over 40 rounds of 82 MM mortar fire. An recoyless rifle an small arms fire. Boy its really getting bad over here. We spotted six tanks an two choppers yesterday. Where about two clicks from Cambodia now. Boy I'm glad Im getting out of the field.

I go on RR in Dec.

Im going to meet my wife in Hawaii. "Wow" fun time.

Revenewers in the hospital with Malaria.

An Polite whent to Japan. An I'm out of the field now. So the only one who's in the gun squad now is Cliff. And he's having trouble with his eyes.

I'm going to take you up on that tour of Portland. Ill call you from fort Lewis on April 27th. You'll haft to keep me from raping women. "Hee Hee" Because I'll sure be horny. You know what its like over here. Remember the alamo boy that was really some place. But know matter where we whent we always had our shit together. Well most of the time. Well doc thats about all I have on this end. Oh before I forget did you ever get those pictures of the alamo I'd sure like to have coppies made. I'll see them when I come to your place.

Give my love to the family.

Your G.I. buddy,

Tweety Bird

Collaborator's comment: The Alamo is mentioned in Jackson's

letters as one of their hilltop bases. He's not sure what adventures he shared with Tweety Bird there. I asked whether he ever paid for sex with a woman over there, and he said, "I take the Fifth." I asked him what it would it cost if a guy did pay for sex there. "It was the equivalent of four dollars."

Regarding the deaths of Preacher and Jim Humphrey, Jackson later got more information. Jackson had mentioned Preacher in one of the letters in which he complains about accomplished people being wasted in Vietnam. He wrote that Preacher was a licensed minister who had to walk point when Steve Gardner didn't. He says that Jim Humphrey was a mild-mannered guy who didn't smoke or drink and who had never had a woman.

Preacher and Jim and the Hawaiian were on patrol. Preacher was the RTO that day (radio transmitter operator), so he was wearing a radio in a backpack. They got ambushed by gooks and Humphrey was killed right away. Preacher took longer to die, because he was shot from behind and the radio absorbed some of the impact. The Hawaiian killed the gooks who ambushed them with his M16. Even though he was treated as a hero, the Hawaiian refused to go on another patrol.

When Jackson went to visit The Wall in Washington, D.C. he found and photographed the name "James G. Humphrey" amidst the names of those killed. He never knew the Preacher's true name.

◇◇◇◇◇

» **Their Delta Company had 87 killed in action and 49 wounded in action.**
» **Tweety Bird had been safely transferred before that disaster.**
» **Tweety Bird is short - 10 more days.**

[Undated]

Hi Cunt,

It's about time you write.

Well Doc, how the hell are you. I'm fine. Well I guess as fine as a guy can be for being over here. I think you know what I mean. I'm hungrey for a peace of ass, that has round eyes. I recieved another one of your letters today.

So you weren't kidding about that devorse. I can't believe it.

I don't know if I told you this but I'm in another unit now.

Boy I'm glad I got out of the first of the 35 infrantry.

Last week Delta company had 87 KIA [killed in action] and 49 W.I.A. [wounded in action]. As soon as I get the death paper I'll write an tell you how many of the old guys made it. I hope Cliff & Lanky are alright.

Collaborator's comment: Jackson did not know Cliff's last name, but he found a Clifford on the Washington, D.C. Wall who died on the date of this battle, so he thinks Cliff probably died.

Well, doc only 10 more days and the war will be over for me. "Short." I never thought I'd see the day I could say that an mean it. Well doc, I'v got to go fuck over some lifers minds.

Write soon.

Your Buddy

Collaborator's comment: Jackson found out more details. Delta Company, the 1st of the 35th, got wiped out in or near Cambodia at Rat Hill. There was a new colonel in command, and he wouldn't allow them to call in air support. They were ambushed with 87 KIA and 49 WIA, as stated in Tweety Bird's letter. They were pinned down and desperately needed air support. Jackson says:

> If I'd been there I'd have had my cross hairs on that colonel.

> I was fortunate to be there at a time when we had maximum air support. We had Puff the Magic Dragon protecting us at night. I remember sitting on a rock on a hillside, and I thought Puff would be flying below where I was, when bullets came close over my head. I saw a wall of red coming right at me.

Collaborator's comment: Tweety Bird and Jackson had some contact after the war, and Jackson believes he might live in the Washington, D.C. area. Jackson tried unsuccessfully to locate Delta Polite. He located Jim Humphrey's name on The Wall in Washington, D.C., and thinks he might have found Clifford's name there. He has lost track of his hometown friend, Steve Gardner, but he formed new friendships with Vietnam vets during his activity to support the fundraising and design of the Oregon Vietnam Veterans Memorial. But with the apathy that accompanies Parkinson's, he has let those friendships slide.

Jackson's entire life has been affected by post-traumatic stress disorder, and he acknowledges it, and has even gone to counseling at Portland's Vet Center. When asked how he would describe his post-traumatic stress, Jackson was able to answer without hesitation:

> I have dreams about Vietnam. The most common one is being in a small launch. My friends and family are with me. The launch gets beached in Vietnam and I think, "How did I get here again? I got kids now." I still have this dream once in awhile. The terror is palpable.

> Over there, you couldn't tell friend from foe. I can no longer trust most people.

> I have resentment, anger, and belligerence. I hate people in authority. I know more than anybody in authority knows about life, death, staying alive, and suffering. I would say to them, "Make me a deal and tell me something I don't already know."

Collaborator's comment: Jackson then mentions the loss of his .45 with its holster with the star on it that came off the body of a dead Viet Cong. It was seized inadvertently by Portland police when they were seizing somebody else's property that the gun was in. He never got his gun back, and he resents them for taking it.

> But I'm still a good shot. I can hit a Coke can by that tree over there.

Not bad for a man with Parkinson's!

> I have a totally changed attitude toward society and its ability to police or govern itself. In our 7,000 years of human history, we've never successfully policed or governed ourselves. I'm like the Indian giving his finger to the oncoming train.

Collaborator's comment: Jackson refers here to an old legal case of mine — until retirement I was a lawyer — that he remembered for thirty years, in which a Native American stood on a railroad track and displayed his middle finger to an oncoming train, then failed to jump off the tracks in time and was killed. Jackson admired the symbolism of the Indian's defiance of encroaching technology.

> Over there, I learned to react instantly to any threat. Hypersensitivity is how you survive over there. My quick response to threat is defensive. It protects me. But it's a sign of PTSD. It doesn't work well in civilian life to react strongly to every sense of threat.

But my faith has helped me calm down a lot. I'm spirit led now, so I don't need to react so much.

And one thing good that I got from being over there is my drive for life. I'm a survivor. I was determined to make it. I got home and saw people endangering their lives with drugs and such, and I couldn't understand it. No matter what, I want to live. Even in this wheelchair. I've heard that some people get so bad with Parkinson's that they want to use doctor-assisted suicide. I can't imagine that for myself. I've worked too hard to stay alive. Vietnam gave me my drive for life.

◇◇◇◇◇

A Word About Parkinson's Disease

Here is a definition of Parkinson's Disease from the Mayo Clinic at http://is.gd/Parkinsons

Parkinson's disease is a progressive disorder of the nervous system that affects your movement. It develops gradually, sometimes starting with a barely noticeable tremor in just one hand. But while a tremor may be the most well-known sign of Parkinson's disease, the disorder also commonly causes stiffness or slowing of movement.

In the early stages of Parkinson's disease, your face may show little or no expression or your arms may not swing when you walk. Your speech may become soft or slurred. Parkinson's disease symptoms worsen as your condition progresses over time.

Although Parkinson's disease can't be cured, medications may markedly improve your symptoms. In occasional cases, your doctor may suggest surgery to regulate certain regions of your brain and improve your symptoms.

One symptom not mentioned in this Mayo Clinic summary, and often one of the first symptoms of Parkinson's, is loss of the sense of smell. Jackson lost his sense of smell many years before his Parkinson's was diagnosed. This collaborator recalls how, when his children were young, Jackson would have them sniff the milk carton to test for freshness because he could not smell sour milk. Years later, when he had developed noticeable tremors and a slow gait, one of the diagnostic tests involved blindfolding him and having him identify scents. It was discovered that he could not smell coffee. With the lack of sense of smell comes lack of sense of taste. He has been underweight with little appetite for many years. Thirty years ago he told this collaborator that he knew when it was time to eat only because his stomach began to hurt. But sweet food pleases him, and he enjoys a nightly snack of pastry.

Medications to calm the tremors were effective for some time, but Jackson eventually became so exhausted from constant shaking, that surgery called "deep brain stimulation" was recommended. A thin wire was surgically inserted into the base of the brain and then run under the skin down to the chest, where a battery pack inserted under the skin delivers electric pulses directly to the brain. It is not known why this works, but when it works well, it does an excellent job of stopping the tremors. Jackson has benefited from DBS for several years, and his shaking is hardly noticeable.

But tremors are not his only symptom. He can still walk, but his gait is stiff and slow, and his balance is untrustworthy so he uses a cane. He can manage one or two steps but not a flight of stairs. He goes into his walk-in closet to dress himself, and he has an accessible shower with no rim to step over, so he can bathe himself and also Eli, who enjoys being scrubbed and showered. He speaks in a soft voice, just above a whisper. His facial expression is difficult to read because it is hard to tell if he is happy or sad when his face reacts to emotion. This is because his facial muscles produce only one dramatic grimace-like expression. He can feed himself, but needs help cutting up meat, because fine motor coordination in the hands is gone. He does almost no handwriting, nor does he use a computer. Music, movies, and watching the nightly news entertain him, but his main entertainment involves sitting on his porch and watching the bustle of farm activities that swirl around him. He considers getting out his painting supplies which are stored in the garage, but with no fine motor coordination, he would have to completely change his artistic style to large brushwork.

He needs to eat food that is easy to chew and to swallow. His mental alertness seems not too affected, and his memory is good and his wry sense of humor fully intact. He can negotiate his electric wheelchair like a Nascar driver, and he can direct the activities that his family does both for him and for the upkeep of his home. For a long time he could drive his accessible van, but now when he goes out he is driven. He has an eagle eye for how money is being spent by his family/caregivers. With reading glasses, he can read books and the Bible. Apathy is a symptom of his Parkinson's that can be difficult for caregivers, because he shows little enthusiasm, and it can be hard to tell what he wants when he works so hard to be amiable and not demanding.

His response to the call of "Medic!" has slowed, but it is still there. One morning, this collaborator was checking on the chicken food in the coop and got attacked by the rooster which tunneled deeply into my fingers with its beak. Early in the morning, with tears in my eyes and blood dripping from my hands, I awoke Doc Jackson by calling, "Medic!," because I assumed that would get his attention and I promptly needed bandages for the profuse bleeding. At first he was confused, but quickly awoke and reacted appropriately to the medical emergency. (Later, one finger unsurprisingly became infected from the animal bite and was successfully treated at Urgent Care with antibiotics.)

For many years the Veterans Administration denied any link between exposure to the toxic defoliant Agent Orange and the many diseases that became common among Vietnam Veterans, including Parkinson's. Now they have come to acknowledge many of the links they had previously denied.

Here is information from the U.S. Department of Veterans Affairs website:

Parkinson's Disease and Agent Orange: Veterans who develop Parkinson's disease and were exposed to Agent Orange or other herbicides during military service do not have to prove a connection between their disease and service to be eligible to receive VA health care and disability compensation.

http://is.gd/AOParkinsons

After many years of denying veterans' claims that Agent Orange caused their Parkinson's, on August 31, 2010 the Veterans Administration promulgated an amended rule in the Federal Registry, acknowledging that there is a presumptive connection between Parkinson's and Agent Orange. http://is.gd/acknowledge

The VA acknowledges that soldiers who served on the ground in Vietnam between 1962 and 1975 were exposed to Agent Orange, due to its widespread use to remove foliage that provided cover for the enemy. http://is.gd/AOExposure

◇◇◇◇◇

Vietnam Veterans
Against the War:

http://is.gd/VVATW

Doc Jackson was not a joiner, so he returned home and tried to get his life on track by going to college, getting an architecture degree, and contributing his skills as a project manager to private and public businesses. Like many traumatized veterans, he kept his mouth shut about the war. So when he wrote in one of his letters that "a protest is forming. I feel it coming on," he was referring to his personal sense of outrage. Just the day before, he had seen Enlisted Man (Echo Mike) Johnson step on an I.E.D., and "it rained body parts." He drafted a letter to his Senator about the reasons the war was bad, but he never joined a formal anti-war protest group. His need for privacy was intense, and his personal protest of refusing to board the plane had only caused him to be court-martialed, with no no benefit to others. It is understandable why he shrank from being seen publicly as a protestor.

But many other veterans publicly protested the war. More than 80,000 Vietnam veterans eventually joined Vietnam Veterans Against the War, an organization that was just starting at the time Jackson served and that grew until their voices gave great legitimacy to the anti-war movement in the early 1970s. Many soldiers felt shame about following dishonorable orders that resulted in civilian deaths so that the enemy body counts could be inflated (such as happened in the shocking My Lai massacre of all the women, children and old people in the village of My Lai), and about following orders to destroy peasants' rice crops to keep them from feeding the Viet Cong. More and more soldiers began to bring the wrongs of U.S. policy to public attention. They taught that a person could protest the war without blaming the warriors, and that even citizens who opposed the war should support the troops. As the war dragged on, the pro-Nam lifers that Jackson and Tweety Bird complained about became the minority.

Like the Hawaiian that Tweety Bird mentioned, who refused to go on another patrol after he killed the men who had ambushed and killed his buddies, and like Jackson, who refused to perform any more "cheap chores" when he was about to go home, many uniformed soldiers began to refuse orders to participate.

In 1971, Colonel Heinl, a Marine historian, wrote in the influential *Armed Forces Journal*:

"The morale, discipline and battle worthiness of the US Armed Forces are, with a few salient exceptions, lower and worse than at any time in this century and possibly in the history of the United States.

"By every conceivable indicator, our army that now remains in Vietnam is in a state approaching collapse, with individual units avoiding or having refused combat, murdering their officers and non-commissioned officers, drug-ridden, and dispirited where not near mutinous..."

One of the antiwar slogans was, "What if they gave a war and nobody came?" Jackson had tried his best not to come, but was pressured by the threat of years of incarceration. But for many others, not participating began to happen. Not only were more and more draftees fleeing to Canada or otherwise avoiding deployment, but the soldiers in the field were refusing orders, and they were "fragging" dangerously gung ho superior officers by killing them with fragmentation grenades — just as Jackson had so calmly threatened to do to the fellows who stole his platoon's beer. They had made these young men "Army Strong," and it was backfiring on the military leadership.

President Richard Nixon became aware that he was Commander in Chief of a fighting force that refused to fight. One theory about the end of U.S. involvement in Vietnam is that President Nixon knew that he had to withdraw U.S. troops because, by 1973, so many refused to go into battle. So Nixon declared a disingenuous "peace with honor," withdrew U.S. troops, and left the South Vietnamese to fall to the communists in April of 1975.

The U.S. Department of Veterans Affairs reports the following statistics and facts at http://is.gd/VAstatistics:

In May of 1968, the US began peace negotiations, which eventually broke down. However, a change in US policy led to the greater emphasis on training and supplying South Vietnamese troops, and US withdrawal began in July 1968.

Collaborator's comment: The May 1968 peace negotiations were the ones Jackson complained of, because they prevented them from attacking the enemy as it resupplied itself during the "peace ceasefire."

Approximately 2,700,000 (two million, seven hundred thousand) American men and women served in Vietnam.

U.S. deaths and missing in action listed on The Vietnam Veterans Memorial in Washington D.C. total more than 58,200.

It was the first time America failed to welcome its veterans back as heroes.

◇◇◇◇◇

Environmental hazards and common diseases:

Pesticide and herbicide spraying was commonplace.

Bacterial and fungal infections of the feet were a major cause of temporary disability.

Skin disease was a leading cause of outpatient visits and hospitalization.

Disease accounted for 70.6% of all hospital admissions with the remaining approximately equally divided between battle casualties (15.6%) and non-battle injury (13.8%).

Collaborator's comment: This non-battle injury figure, which approaches the percentage of battle injuries, is in accord with Jackson's reports of multiple accidents, such as his own sprained ankle when he fell into a ditch, or his finger injured from a machete handle, or the self-inflicted machete wound to one of his men's legs, and the near disaster when a DET cord explosion sent a flying tree toward Gardner, plus many near disasters from men stumbling around drunk at night.

40,000 cases of Malaria were reported.

Diarrheal diseases were also common.

◇◇◇◇◇

Glossary of G.I. Slang and Abbreviations Used in Doc's Letters Home

A.P.C.
Armored Personnel Carrier

A.P.O.
Army Post Office

ARVN
Army of Vietnam, meaning the southern, friendly forces working with the United States.

Beother or Be-other
Not G.I. slang, but a family term of endearment. When kid sister Jodi was little, she couldn't say "brother," so she called Jerome her "beother" (pronounced bee-other). He often signs his letters this way.

Charlie
An enemy soldier, either a Viet Cong guerilla or a North Vietnamese soldier with the regular army.

Chopper
A helicopter, usually one of four types: The Chinook (also

219

called a Shit Hook) was a large, double rotor helicopter for heavy lifting and for transporting "ass and trash" (people and supplies); The Huey (also called a Slick) was used for dropping supplies to troops, transporting them, and for picking up the injured from combat zones; The LOTCH was a light observation helicopter for viewing the conditions on the ground; and The Cobra was a narrow Slick in which one pilot sits behind the other. There are no door gunners. Made for fast and powerful minigun and rocket attacks.

Click
Kilometer

CMB
The coveted Combat Medics Badge was awarded to Jackson for performing medical duties while attached to an infantry unit engaged in active ground combat while he was personally present and under fire. Code of Federal Regulations §587.70.

C.Q.
Charge of Quarters. Somebody must always be awake at Army quarters, and the person assigned to stay awake all night is the C.Q.

Dee Dee Mau
Approximation of Vietnamese for "go away, get out of here."

D.R.O.S.
Date Returned from OverSeas.

E.T.S.
Elapsed Time of Service (discharge date).

The First Thing Smoking:
Usually a helicopter, or maybe a truck. Transportation out.

Frag
Killing somebody with a fragmentation grenade. Troops some-times killed their own commanding officers this way if the officers gave stupid, life-threatening orders.

Going hunting
In this context, it refers to a search and destroy mission to seek out the enemy, kill him, and add him to the U.S.'s body count.

Gooks
Casually used derogatory slang for the enemy forces, also called dinks or Charlie. Charlie is from the code phrase "Victor Charlie," which stands for V.C., i.e., meaning the Viet Cong.

Ho Chi Minh
Leader of the northern military forces who was determined to reunite the divided Vietnam under anti-colonial communist rule and to drive out U.S. imperialist influence in the South. The country had been divided in the 1950s by the French colo-nialists, with U.S. backing, in order to provide a non-commu-nist buffer state in S.E. Asia.

Ho Chi Minh Trail
A web of north to south trails and dirt roads, many in neigh-boring Laos, on which communist forces moved troops, weap-ons, and supplies into South Vietnam.

Hooch
A hut or an improvised shelter in the field.

I.E.D.
Improvised Explosive Device.

In country
In Vietnam.

L.B.J.
U.S. President Lyndon Baines Johnson

L.B.J. — alternate meaning
Lon Bin Jail, the place where the lieutenant that Jackson refers to as Dufus kept threatening to send him for insubordination. Jackson would reply, "Promises, promises."

Lifer
Derogatory term for a permanent member of the armed forces, as opposed to draftees and enlistees who served a set time until discharge. Lifers were more likely than draftees to be pro-war, and it was feared that, by being too gung ho, they put others at risk unnecessarily.

L.Z.
A cleared area used as a Landing Zone for helicopters; also used to refer to a temporary base camp.

MARS station
Military Assistance Radio Station, where the soldiers talk on a ham radio and volunteers relay the radio message to the States.

MASH
Mobile Army Surgical Hospital.

Med-Cap or MEDCAP
Taking about medicine to villagers under the Medical Civilian Assistance Program. This was the Vietnam War era attempt to "win the hearts and minds of the people."

Medivac
Medical evacuations of injured and sick soldiers was done by calling in helicopters to medivac the soldier out of the field. Choppers landing at a battlefield were always at great risk, and chopper pilots were honored and admired.

Number 1
The best or great, as in "I got a number 1 shower."

N.V.A.
North Vietnamese Army, one of the two enemy communist forces. The other was the Viet Cong.

The Oasis
A base with a munitions depot on the way to Ban Me Thuot.

Port Call
The place where you pick up an overseas flight.

PTSD
Post-Traumatic Stress Disorder is a neurological change in the brain that occurs after experiencing a sudden stressful event such as combat, an earthquake, or a tornado. It is characterized by hypersensitivity to threat, and it is usually permanent, but there are methods to learn to cope with it.

R&R
Rest and Recreation.

Round eyes
Non-Asian woman.

Short
A short time remaining until return to the states.

TET
The TET offensive took place in the winter months of 1968. It started during the Vietnamese New Year celebration, called TET. The North Vietnamese Army and the Viet Cong surprised everyone with a massive, coordinated attack simultaneously on all the major populated areas in South Vietnam. The U.S. lost more than 4,000 soldiers in only a couple of months. The North seized and held the town of Hue for more than a month, but eventually they were pushed back from the towns, and the fighting resumed as before, in the jungles.

Viet Cong
Non-uniformed communist guerilla fighters who blended in with the local populace making it impossible to tell friend from foe.

Walk point
On patrol, it was dangerous walking through the jungle. The enemy booby trapped the woods in many clever ways, so one person would always be assigned to walk first, called walking point. Point was the most dangerous position.

Un-ass the A.O.
Remove a person or people from the area of operation. Depopulate. A man might throw a fragmentation grenade in order to "un-ass the A.O."

The Wall
Common name for the impressive Vietnam Veterans Memorial in Washington, D.C. that commemorates all U.S. Forces lost in that conflict, listing each person by name.

The world
Back home. Not Vietnam.